The Prentice Hall
Classic Short Prose Reader

■ ■ ■

Pamela Farvolden
University of Alberta

Paul Lumsden
Grant MacEwan College

Prentice
Hall

Toronto

To our families.

Canadian Cataloguing in Publication Data

The Prentice Hall classic short prose reader

ISBN 0-13-028331-2

1. College readers. 2. English language – Rhetoric – Problems, exercises, etc. I. Farvolden, Pamela, 1957– . II. Lumsden, Paul, 1961– . III. Title: Classic short prose reader.

PE1417.P73 2002   808'.0427   C2001-930040-9

ISBN 0-13-028331-2

Vice President, Editorial Director: Michael Young
Editor-in-Chief: David Stover
Signing Representative: Andrew Wellner
Associate Editor: Meaghan Eley
Senior Production Editor: Sherry Torchinsky
Copy Editor: Pam Young
Production Coordinator: Peggy Brown
Page Layout: Janette Thompson (Jansom)
Art Director: Mary Opper
Cover and Interior Design: Sarah Battersby
Cover Image: Artville

1 2 3 4 5   05 04 03 02 01

Printed and bound in Canada.

CONTENTS

■ ─────────────────────────────── ■

Alphabetical by Author

CONTENTS

Alphabetically by Title

PREFACE

This anthology grew out of our desire for a short, affordable collection of familiar essays: essays which have been read and reprinted many times since their first publication and which have been taught and continue to be taught regularly in Canadian university classrooms. We wanted our collection to be short because we (and, often, our students) have felt keenly the lack of an affordable, practical anthology suitable not only for courses which centre on the study of the essay but also for undergraduate survey courses of which studying the essay as a genre is often only a part.

Our main principle of selection has been familiarity: we have included those essays which we return to again and again in our teaching; which students remember, whether they love them or hate them; which have become, or are on their way to becoming, classics of the genre. And these essays do indeed fit all three of the main senses given in the *Oxford English Dictionary* for the adjective *classic:* they are all of the highest quality, the first class; they are all good and important examples of their kind; and they all exhibit enduring worth—their appeal and application seem timeless. Any process of selecting from a body of excellent work, however bound by principles of selection, is nevertheless inherently subjective; but we hope that subjectivity has been mitigated by the regularity with which most of these selections have appeared in print, and by our informal conversations with our colleagues.

We have also aimed for variety within this relatively short collection. For example, though many of the selections are from the twentieth century, readers will also find essays from the seventeenth to the nineteenth centuries. And they will find writing on a variety of subjects from British, American, and Canadian men and women.

The strength of our text lies in this combination of brevity, familiarity, and variety. Each essay is introduced with information about its writer and the context in which it first appeared, and each paragraph is numbered for easy reference, but other pedagogical material is kept to a minimum in order to focus on the essays themselves, some of the best examples of the genre. We hope students and instructors will enjoy this group of classic essays, brought together in an appealing and practical collection, as much as we have enjoyed reading, teaching, and selecting them.

ACKNOWLEDGEMENTS

Thanks are due to many people: our colleagues at the University of Alberta and Grant MacEwan College who listened to and commented on our ideas for this project; Andy Wellner of Pearson Education Canada, who encouraged us to begin; our editors at Pearson Education Canada, who advised us along the way; Luba Slabyj, for some timely research help; and especially our families, who supported and applauded our efforts. To them all, we say a grateful thank-you.

Margaret Atwood

■ ■ ■

Amnesty International: An Address

Margaret Atwood (b. 1939), novelist, poet, essayist, and literary and social critic, is one of Canada's most acclaimed and accomplished writers.
Born in Ottawa, Atwood spent her early years living in remote northern
"bush country," following her father, an entomologist, as he conducted
research. She has a BA from the University of Toronto (1961) and an MA
from Radcliffe (1962). A Fellow of the Royal Society and a Companion of
the Order of Canada, Atwood holds twelve honorary degrees and has
been the recipient of numerous awards and honours for her writing. She
began her career as a poet, winning the Governor-General's award for poetry in 1966 for *The Circle Game*. Three of her nine critically successful novels have won international acclaim and garnered prestigious writing
awards: the Governor-General's award for *The Handmaid's Tale* (1986), the
Giller Prize for *Alias Grace* (1996), and, most recently, the Booker Prize for
The Blind Assassin (2000). Atwood has also written TV and radio scripts
and published several collections of short stories, essays, and literary criticism as well as four children's books. The following essay was first delivered as an address to a world meeting of Amnesty International in
Toronto, 1981.

The subject we have come together to address is one which in-
creases in importance as the giants of this world move closer
and closer to violent and fatal confrontation. Broadly put, it is:
what is the writer's responsibility, if any, to the society in which he
or she lives? The question is not a new one; it's been with us at
least since the time of Plato; but more and more the answers of
the world's governments have taken the form of amputation: of the
tongue, of the soul, of the head. 1

We in Canada are ill-equipped to come to grips even with
the problem, let alone the solution. We live in a society in which
the main consensus seems to be that the artist's duty is to
entertain and divert, nothing more. Occasionally our critics get a
little heavy and start talking about the human condition, but on
the whole the audience prefers art not to be a mirror held up to 2

life but a Disneyland of the soul, containing Romanceland, Spyland, Pornoland and all the other Escapelands which are so much more agreeable than the complex truth. When we take an author seriously, we prefer to believe that her vision derives from her individual and subjective and neurotic tortured soul—we like artists to have tortured souls—not from the world she is looking at. Sometimes our artists believe this version too, and the ego takes over. *I, me* and *mine* are our favourite pronouns; *we, us* and *ours* are low on the list. The artist is not seen as a lens for focusing the world but as a solipsism. We are good at measuring an author's production in terms of his craft. We are not good at analyzing it in terms of his politics, and by and large we do not do so.

By "politics" I do not mean how you voted in the last election, 3 although that is included. I mean who is entitled to do what to whom, with impunity; who profits by it; and who therefore eats what. Such material enters a writer's work not because the writer is or is not consciously political but because a writer is an observer, a witness, and such observations are the air he breathes. They are the air all of us breathe; the only difference is that the author looks, and then writes down what he sees. What he sees will depend on how closely he looks and at what, but look he must.

In some countries, an author is censored not only for what 4 he says but for how he says it, and an unconventional style is therefore a declaration of artistic freedom. Here we are eclectic; we don't mind experimental styles, in fact we devote learned journals to their analysis; but our critics sneer somewhat at anything they consider "heavy social commentary" or—a worse word— "message." Stylistic heavy guns are dandy, as long as they aren't pointed anywhere in particular. We like the human condition as long as it is seen as personal and individual. Placing politics and poetics in two watertight compartments is a luxury, just as specialization of any kind is a luxury, and it is possible only in a society where luxuries abound. Most countries in the world cannot afford such luxuries, and this North American way of thinking is alien to them. It was even alien in North America, not long ago. We've already forgotten that in the 1950's many artists, both in the United States and here, were persecuted solely on the grounds of their presumed politics. Which leads us to another mistaken Canadian belief: the belief that it can't happen here.

It has happened here, many times. Although our country is 5 one of the most peaceful and prosperous on earth, although we do not shoot artists here, although we do not execute political opponents and although this is one of the few remaining countries in which we can have a gathering like this without expecting to be arrested or blown up, we should not overlook the fact that Canada's record on civil rights issues is less than pristine. Our treatment of our native peoples has been shameful. This is the country in which citizens of Japanese origin were interned during the Second World War and had their property stolen (when a government steals property it is called "confiscation"); it is also the country in which thousands of citizens were arrested, jailed and held without warrant or explanation, during the time of the War Measures Act, a scant eleven years ago. There was no general outcry in either case. Worse things have not happened not because we are genetically exempt but because we lead pampered lives.

Our methods of controlling artists are not violent, but they do 6 exist. We control through the marketplace and through critical opinion. We are also controlled by the economics of culture, which in Canada still happen to be those of a colonial branch-plant. In 1960 the number of Canadian books published here was minute, and the numbers sold pathetic. Things have changed very much in twenty years, but Canadian books still account for a mere 25 percent of the overall book trade and paperback books for under 5 percent. Talking about this situation is still considered nationalistic chauvinism. Nevertheless, looked at in the context of the wider picture, I suppose we are lucky to have any percent at all; they haven't yet sent in the Marines and if they do it won't be over books, but over oil.

We in this country should use our privileged position not as 7 a shelter from the world's realities but as a platform from which to speak. Many are denied their voices; we are not. A voice is a gift; it should be cherished and used, to utter fully human speech if possible. Powerlessness and silence go together; one of the first efforts made in any totalitarian takeover is to suppress the writers, the singers, the journalists, those who are the collective voice. Get rid of the union leaders and pervert the legal system and what you are left with is a reign of terror.

As we read the newspapers, we learn we are existing right 8 now in a state of war. The individual wars may not be large and they are being fought far from here, but there is really only one war, that between those who would like the future to be, in the words of George Orwell, a boot grinding forever into a human face, and those who would like it to be a state of something we still dream of as freedom. The battle shifts according to the ground occupied by the enemy. Greek myth tells of a man called Procrustes, who was a great equalizer. He had a system for making all human beings the same size: if they were too small he stretched them, if they were too tall he cut off their feet or their heads. The Procrustes today are international operators, not confined to any one ideology or religion. The world is full of perversions of the notion of equality, just as it is full of perversions of the notion of freedom. True freedom is not being able to do whatever you like to whomever you want to do it to. Freedom that exists as a result of the servitude of others is not true freedom.

The most lethal weapon in the world's arsenals is not the 9
neutron bomb or chemical warfare; but the human mind that devises such things and puts them to use. But it is the human mind also that can summon up the power to resist, that can imagine a better world than the one before it, that can retain memory and courage in the face of unspeakable suffering. Oppression involves a failure of the imagination: the failure to imagine the full humanity of other human beings. If the imagination were a negligible thing and the act of writing a mere frill, as many in this society would like to believe, regimes all over the world would not be at such pains to exterminate them. The ultimate desire of Procrustes is a population of lobotomized zombies. The writer, unless he is a mere word processor, retains three attributes that power-mad regimes cannot tolerate: a human imagination, in the many forms it may take; the power to communicate; and hope. It may seem odd for me to speak of hope in the midst of what many of my fellow Canadians will call a bleak vision, but as the American writer Flannery O'Connor once said, people without hope do not write novels.

Sir Francis Bacon

■ ■ ■

Francis Bacon (1561–1626), statesman, philosopher and essayist, was born in London, England, and educated at Trinity College, Cambridge. At fifteen, he began studying law at Gray's Inn and became a leading lawyer, garnering many appointments: he was knighted in 1602, became Solicitor-General in 1609, Attorney General in 1613, Lord Chancellor in 1618, Baron Verulam in 1618, and Viscount in 1621. In 1621, however, he was found guilty of accepting bribes and stripped of his offices. He spent the rest of his life writing both scientific treatises and what we have come to know as the personal essay.

Although trained as a lawyer, Bacon was much interested in science, and he is credited with popularizing the application of induction to scientific inquiry. He also made a significant contribution to literature, creating the essay as an English language literary genre. Inspired by the *Essais* (1580) of France's Michel Montaigne, Bacon wrote *Essays or Counsels, Civil and Moral* (1597), a work he revised and expanded in 1612 and again in 1625. Short and aphoristic, these "meditations" were meant to be useful, moral, and thought-provoking treatments of both concrete and abstract subjects. The following essays combine homely wisdom with rhetorical skill and technique, and are often reprinted.

Of Marriage and Single Life

He that hath wife and children hath given hostages to fortune; for they are impediments to great enterprises, either of virtue or mischief. Certainly the best works, and of greatest merit for the public, have proceeded from the unmarried or childless men; which both in affection and means have married and endowed the public. Yet it were great reason that those that have children should have greatest care of future times; unto which they know they must transmit their dearest pledges. Some there are, who though they lead a single life, yet their thoughts do end with themselves, and account future times impertinences. Nay, there are some other, that account wife and children but as bills of charges. Nay more, there are some foolish rich covetous men, that take a pride in having no children, because they may be thought so much the richer. For perhaps they have heard some talk, *Such an one is a great rich man,* and another except to it, *Yea, but he hath a great charge of children;* as if it were an abatement to his riches. But the most ordinary cause of a single life is liberty, especially in certain self-pleasing and humorous minds, which are so sensible of every restraint, as they will go near to think their girdles and garters to be bonds and shackles. Unmarried men are best friends, best masters, best servants; but not always best subjects; for they are light to run away; and almost all fugitives are of that condition. A single life doth well with churchmen; for charity will hardly water the ground where it must first fill a pool. It is indifferent for judges and magistrates; for if they be facile and corrupt, you shall have a servant five times worse than a wife. For soldiers, I find the generals commonly in their hortatives put men in mind of their wives and children; and I think the despising of marriage amongst the Turks maketh the vulgar soldier more base. Certainly wife and children are a kind of discipline of humanity; and single men, though they may be many times more charitable, because their means are less exhaust, yet, on the other side, they are more cruel and hard-hearted, (good to make severe inquisitors,) because their tenderness is not so oft called upon. Grave natures, led by custom, and therefore constant, are commonly loving husbands, as was said of Ulysses, *Vetulam suam prœtulit immortalitati.*[1] Chaste women are often proud and froward, as presuming upon the merit of their chastity. It is one of the best bonds both of chastity and obedience in the wife, if she think her husband wise; which she will never do if she find him jealous. Wives are young men's mistresses; companions for middle age; and old men's nurses. So as a man may have a quarrel to marry when he will. But yet he was reputed one of the wise men, that made answer to the question, when a man should marry?—*A young man not yet, an elder man not at all.* It is often seen that bad husbands have very good wives; whether it be that it raiseth the price of their husband's kindness when it comes; or that the wives take a pride in their patience. But this never fails, if the bad husbands were of their own choosing, against their friends' consent; for then they will be sure to make good their own folly.

---

[1] He preferred his old wife to immortality. Homer, *Odyssey* V, 218.

Of Studies

Studies serve for delight, for ornament, and for ability. Their 1 chief use for delight, is in privateness and retiring; for ornament, is in discourse; and for ability, is in the judgment and disposition of business. For expert men can execute, and perhaps judge of particulars, one by one; but the general counsels, and the plots and marshalling of affairs, come best from those that are learned. To spend too much time in studies is sloth; to use them too much for ornament, is affectation; to make judgment wholly by their rules, is the humour of a scholar. They perfect nature, and are perfected by experience: for natural abilities are like natural plants, that need proyning by study; and studies themselves do give forth directions too much at large, except they be bounded in by experience. Crafty men contemn studies, simple men admire them, and wise men use them; for they teach not their own use; but that is a wisdom without them, and above them, won by observation. Read not to contradict and confute; nor to believe and take for granted; nor to find talk and discourse; but to weigh and consider. Some books are to be tasted, others to be swallowed, and some few to be chewed and digested; that is, some books are to be read only in parts; others to be read, but not curiously; and some few to be read wholly, and with diligence and attention. Some books also may be read by deputy, and extracts made of them by others; but that would be only in the less important arguments, and the meaner sort of books; else distilled books are like common distilled waters, flashy things. Reading maketh a full man; conference a ready man; and writing an exact man. And therefore, if a man write little, he had need have a great memory; if he confer little, he had need have a present wit: and if he read little, he had need have much cunning, to seem to know that he doth not. Histories make men wise; poets witty; the mathematics subtile; natural philosophy deep; moral grave; logic and rhetoric able to contend. *Abeunt studia in mores.*[2] Nay there is no stond or impediment in the wit, but may be wrought out by fit studies: like as diseases of the body may have appropriate exercises. Bowling is good for the stone and reins; shooting for the lungs and breast;

---

[2] Studies pass over into manners. Ovid, *Heroides* XV, 83.

gentle walking for the stomach; riding for the head; and the like. So if a man's wit be wandering, let him study the mathematics; for in demonstrations, if his wit be called away never so little, he must begin again. If his wit be not apt to distinguish or find differences, let him study the schoolmen; for they are *cymini sectores*.[3] If he be not apt to beat over matters, and to call up one thing to prove and illustrate another, let him study the lawyers' cases. So every defect of the mind may have a special receipt.

---

[3] splitters of hairs

Judy Brady

■■■

Why I Want a Wife

Judy Brady (b. 1937), feminist, social activist, writer, was born in San Francisco and has a BFA in painting from the University of Iowa. Active in the women's liberation movement of the late 1960s, she left it in the 1970s, feeling it had been watered down. In 1973 she made the first of several trips to Cuba, where she gained a heightened awareness of racism, classism, and imperialism, writing an article about the Cuban educational system, which was published in *Radical Teacher*. In 1980, Brady was diagnosed with breast cancer and since then has been active in raising political, cultural, and social awareness of this disease. She edited and contributed to the book *1 in 3: Women with Cancer Confront an Epidemic* (Cleis Press, 1991), her attempt to use women's personal experience to raise serious questions about how we think of cancer in this culture. Since then, she has spoken widely about the politics of cancer and publishes a regular column in the series "Cashing In On Cancer" for the newsletter of the Women's Cancer Resource Center in Berkeley. She is on the board of Greenaction, a local environmental justice organization, and does volunteer training in the politics of cancer. Brady may be best known, however, for the following essay, which, with its provocative discussion of marriage roles, is one of the most frequently reprinted essays of the last few decades. "Why I Want a Wife" was first published as "I Want a Wife" in the preview issue of *Ms.* magazine, Spring 1972.[1]

I belong to that classification of people known as wives. I am A Wife. And, not altogether incidentally, I am a mother.   1

Not too long ago a male friend of mine appeared on the scene fresh from a recent divorce. He had one child, who is, of course, with his ex-wife. He is looking for another wife. As I thought about him while I was ironing one evening, it suddenly occurred to me that I, too, would like to have a wife. Why do I want a wife?   2

I would like to go back to school so that I can become economically independent, support myself, and, if need be,   3

---

[1]We are grateful to Ms. Brady for providing much of this biographical information.

support those dependent upon me. I want a wife who will work and send me to school. And while I am going to school I want a wife to take care of my children. I want a wife to keep track of the children's doctor and dentist appointments. And to keep track of mine, too. I want a wife to make sure my children eat properly and are kept clean. I want a wife who will wash the children's clothes and keep them mended. I want a wife who is a good nurturant attendant to my children, who arranges for their schooling, makes sure that they have an adequate social life with their peers, takes them to the park, the zoo, etc. I want a wife who takes care of the children when they are sick, a wife who arranges to be around when the children need special care, because, of course, I cannot miss classes at school. My wife must arrange to lose time at work and not lose the job. It may mean a small cut in my wife's income from time to time, but I guess I can tolerate that. Needless to say, my wife will arrange and pay for the care of the children while my wife is working.

I want a wife who will take care of *my* physical needs. I want 4 a wife who will keep my house clean. A wife who will pick up after me. I want a wife who will keep my clothes clean, ironed, mended, replaced when need be, and who will see to it that my personal things are kept in their proper place so that I can find what I need the minute I need it. I want a wife who cooks the meals, a wife who is a *good* cook. I want a wife who will plan the menus, do the necessary grocery shopping, prepare the meals, serve them pleasantly, and then do the cleaning up while I do my studying. I want a wife who will care for me when I am sick and sympathize with my pain and loss of time from school. I want a wife to go along when our family takes a vacation so that someone can continue to care for me and my children when I need a rest and change of scene.

I want a wife who will not bother me with rambling 5 complaints about a wife's duties. But I want a wife who will listen to me when I feel the need to explain a rather difficult point I have come across in my course of studies. And I want a wife who will type my papers for me when I have written them.

I want a wife who will take care of the details of my social life. 6 When my wife and I are invited out by friends, I want a wife who will take care of the babysitting arrangements. When I meet people at school that I like and want to entertain, I want a wife who will have the house clean, will prepare a special meal, serve it to me and my friends, and not interrupt when I talk about the things that interest me and my friends. I want a wife who will have arranged that the children are fed and ready for bed before my guests arrive so that the children do not bother us. I want a wife who takes care of the needs of my guests so that they feel comfortable, who makes sure that they have an ashtray, that they are passed the hors d'oeuvres, that they are offered a second helping of the food, that their wine glasses are replenished when necessary, that their coffee is served to them as they like it.

And I want a wife who knows that sometimes I need a night 7
out by myself.

I want a wife who is sensitive to my sexual needs, a wife 8
who makes love passionately and eagerly when I feel like it, a wife who makes sure that I am satisfied. And, of course, I want a wife who will not demand sexual attention when I am not in the mood for it. I want a wife who assumes the complete responsibility for birth control, because I do not want more children. I want a wife who will remain sexually faithful to me so that I do not have to clutter up my intellectual life with jealousies. And I want a wife who understands that *my* sexual needs may entail more than strict adherence to monogamy. I must, after all, be able to relate to people as fully as possible.

If, by chance, I find another person more suitable as a wife 9
than the wife I already have, I want the liberty to replace my present wife with another one. Naturally, I will expect a fresh, new life; my wife will take the children and be solely responsible for them so that I am left free.

When I am through with school and have a job, I want my 10
wife to quit working and remain at home so that my wife can more fully and completely take care of a wife's duties.

My God, who *wouldn't* want a wife? 11

Robertson Davies

■ ■ ■

A Few Kind Words for Superstition

Robertson Davies (1913–1995), academic, critic, playwright, essayist, and acclaimed novelist, was born in Thamesville, Ontario, and educated at Queen's University in Kingston, Ontario, and at Balliol College, Oxford, where he earned a Bachelor's degree in 1938. After graduation, he studied, acted, and directed drama at the Old Vic theatre in London, returning to Canada in 1940 to become the literary editor of *Saturday Night* magazine and, later, the editor (1940–55) and publisher (1955–65) of the *Peterborough Examiner*. During this period Davies wrote and produced several plays and also published eighteen books, including his first trilogy of novels, and numerous essays and articles. The humorous essays he wrote for the *Examiner* under the pseudonym Samuel Marchbanks were collected in *The Diary of Samuel Marchbanks* (1947), *The Table Talk of Samuel Marchbanks* (1949), and *Samuel Marchbanks' Almanac* (1967). His plays include *Eros at Breakfast* (winner of the 1948 Dominion Drama Festival Award), *Fortune, My Foe* (1949), and *At My Heart's Core* (1950). In 1960 Davies began his academic career, joining Trinity College at the University of Toronto to teach literature, and becoming master of Massey College in 1963. Davies' reputation rests primarily on his novels. He completed three well-received trilogies and was working on a fourth when he died. His first three novels, *Tempest Tost* (1951), *Leaven of Malice* (1954)—which won the Stephen Leacock Award for Humour—and *A Mixture of Frailties* (1958), known as the Salterton Trilogy, explored central Canadian cultural life. The second group of novels, known as the Deptford Trilogy, is considered his finest work; it includes *Fifth Business* (1970), *The Manticore* (1972)—which won the Governor-General's Award—and *World of Wonders* (1975). The Cornish Trilogy includes *The Rebel Angels* (1981), *What's Bred in the Bone* (1985), and *The Lyre of Orpheus* (1988). His final novels, *Murther and Walking Spirits* (1991) and *The Cunning Man* (1995), were part of a planned fourth trilogy, the Toronto Books. Davies garnered a number of honours and distinctions during his career: the recipient of many honorary degrees, he was made an RSC fellow in 1967 and a Companion of the Order of Canada in 1972. He was also the first Canadian to become an honorary Member of the American Academy and Institute of Arts and Letters. The following essay appeared as a guest column in *Newsweek* magazine on November 20, 1978.

In grave discussions of "the renaissance of the irrational" in our 1
time, superstition does not figure largely as a serious challenge
to reason or science. Parapsychology, UFO's, miracle cures, tran-
scendental meditation and all the paths to instant enlightenment are
condemned, but superstition is merely deplored. Is it because it
has an unacknowledged hold on so many of us?

Few people will admit to being superstitious; it implies naïveté 2
or ignorance. But I live in the middle of a large university, and I
see superstition in its four manifestations, alive and flourishing
among people who are indisputably rational and learned.

You did not know that superstition takes four forms? 3
Theologians assure us that it does. First is what they call Vain
Observances, such as not walking under a ladder, and that kind
of thing. Yet I saw a deeply learned professor of anthropology,
who had spilled some salt, throwing a pinch of it over his left
shoulder; when I asked him why, he replied, with a wink, that it
was "to hit the Devil in the eye." I did not question him further
about his belief in the Devil: but I noticed that he did not smile
until I asked him what he was doing.

Consulting Oracles

The second form is Divination, or consulting oracles. Another 4
learned professor I know, who would scorn to settle a problem by
tossing a coin (which is a humble appeal to Fate to declare itself),
told me quite seriously that he had resolved a matter related to
university affairs by consulting the *I Ching*. And why not? There
are thousands of people on this continent who appeal to the *I
Ching*, and their general level of education seems to absolve them
of superstition. Almost, but not quite. The *I Ching*, to the
embarrassment of rationalists, often gives excellent advice.

The third form is Idolatry, and universities can show plenty 5
of that. If you have ever supervised a large examination room,
you know how many jujus, lucky coins and other bringers of
luck are placed on the desks of the candidates. Modest idolatry,
but what else can you call it?

The fourth form is Improper Worship of the True God. A 6
while ago, I learned that every day, for several days, a $2 bill (in
Canada we have $2 bills, regarded by some people as unlucky)
had been tucked under a candlestick on the altar of a college
chapel. Investigation revealed that an engineering student,
worried about a girl, thought that bribery of the Deity might

help. When I talked with him, he did not think he was pricing
God cheap, because he could afford no more. A reasonable
argument, but perhaps God was proud that week, for the
scientific oracle went against him.

Terror of the Deity

Superstition seems to run, a submerged river of crude 7
religion, below the surface of human consciousness. It has done
so for as long as we have any chronicle of human behavior, and
although I cannot prove it, I doubt if it is more prevalent today
than it has always been. Superstition, the theologians tell us,
comes from the Latin *supersisto*, meaning to stand in terror of the
Deity. Most people keep their terror within bounds, but they
cannot root it out, nor do they seem to want to do so.

The more the teaching of formal religion declines, or takes 8
a sociological form, the less God appears to great numbers of
people as a God of Love, resuming his older form of a watchful,
minatory power, to be placated and cajoled. Superstition makes
its appearance, apparently unbidden, very early in life, when
children fear that stepping on cracks in the sidewalk will bring ill
fortune. It may persist even among the greatly learned and
devout, as in the case of Dr. Samuel Johnson, who felt it necessary
to touch posts that he passed in the street. The psychoanalysts
have their explanation, but calling a superstition a compulsion
neurosis does not banish it.

Many superstitions are so widespread and so old that they 9
must have risen from a depth of the human mind that is
indifferent to race or creed. Orthodox Jews place a charm on their
doorposts; so do (or did) the Chinese. Some peoples of Middle
Europe believe that when a man sneezes, his soul, for that
moment, is absent from his body, and they hasten to bless him,
lest the soul be seized by the Devil. How did the Melanesians
come by the same idea? Superstition seems to have a link with
some body of belief that far antedates the religions we know —
religions which have no place for such comforting little
ceremonies and charities.

People who like disagreeable historical comparisons recall 10
that when Rome was in decline, superstition proliferated wildly,
and that something of the same sort is happening in our Western
world today. They point to the popularity of astrology, and it is
true that sober newspapers that would scorn to deal in love
philters carry astrology columns and the fashion magazines count

them among their most popular features. But when has astrology not been popular? No use saying science discredits it. When has the heart of man given a damn for science?

Superstition in general is linked to man's yearning to know his   11 fate, and to have some hand in deciding it. When my mother was a child, she innocently joined her Roman Catholic friends in killing spiders on July 11, until she learned that this was done to ensure heavy rain the day following, the anniversary of the Battle of the Boyne, when the Orangemen would hold their parade. I knew an Italian, a good scientist, who watched every morning before leaving his house, so that the first person he met would not be a priest or a nun, as this would certainly bring bad luck.

The Lucky Baby

I am not one to stand aloof from the rest of humanity in this   12 matter, for when I was a university student, a gypsy woman with a child in her arms used to appear every year at examination time, and ask a shilling of anyone who touched the Lucky Baby; that swarthy infant cost me four shillings altogether, and I never failed an examination. Of course, I did it merely for the joke— or so I thought then. Now, I am humbler.

Joan Didion

■ ■ ■

Why I Write

Joan Didion (b. 1934), journalist, essayist, screenwriter, and novelist, was born in Sacramento, California, and graduated from the University of California at Berkeley in 1956. After winning an essay prize sponsored by *Vogue* magazine, she went to New York and worked for *Vogue* between 1956 and 1963, eventually becoming an associate editor. She has contributed articles and columns to a variety of magazines. Didion's precise, lucid prose style has made her an acclaimed novelist and essayist. A partial list of novels includes her first, *Run River* (1963), *Play It as It Lays* (1970), for which she was nominated for a National Book Award, *A Book of Common Prayer* (1977), and, most recently, *The Last Thing He Wanted* (1996). Her first essay collection was *Slouching toward Bethlehem* (1968); other collections include *The White Album* (1979), *Salvador* (1983), *Miami* (1987), and *After Henry* (1992). She has also collaborated with her husband John Gregory Dunne on several screenplays. The following essay is based on a lecture Didion gave at the University of California at Berkeley; it was first published in *The New York Times Book Review* in December 1976.

O f course I stole the title for this talk, from George Orwell. One 1
reason I stole it was that I like the sound of the words: *Why I Write*. There you have three short unambiguous words that share a sound, and the sound they share is this:

I

I

I

In many ways writing is the act of saying *I*, of imposing 2
oneself upon other people, of saying *listen to me, see it my way, change your mind*. It's an aggressive, even a hostile act. You can disguise its aggressiveness all you want with veils of subordinate clauses and qualifiers and tentative subjunctives, with ellipses and evasions—with the whole manner of intimating rather than claiming, of alluding rather than stating—but there's no getting around the fact that setting words on paper is the tactic of a secret

bully, an invasion, an imposition of the writer's sensibility on the reader's most private space.

I stole the title not only because the words sounded right but 3 because they seemed to sum up, in a no-nonsense way, all I have to tell you. Like many writers I have only this one "subject," this one "area": the act of writing. I can bring you no reports from any other front. I may have other interests: I am "interested," for example, in marine biology, but I don't flatter myself that you would come out to hear me talk about it. I am not a scholar. I am not in the least an intellectual, which is not to say that when I hear the word "intellectual" I reach for my gun, but only to say that I do not think in abstracts. During the years when I was an undergraduate at Berkeley, I tried, with a kind of hopeless late-adolescent energy, to buy some temporary visa into the world of ideas, to forge for myself a mind that could deal with the abstract.

In short I tried to think. I failed. My attention veered 4 inexorably back to the specific, to the tangible, to what was generally considered, by everyone I knew then and for that matter have known since, the peripheral. I would try to contemplate the Hegelian dialectic and would find myself concentrating instead on a flowering pear tree outside my window and the particular way the petals fell on my floor. I would try to read linguistic theory and would find myself wondering instead if the lights were on in the bevatron up the hill. When I say that I was wondering if the lights were on in the bevatron you might immediately suspect, if you deal in ideas at all, that I was registering the bevatron as a political symbol, thinking in shorthand about the military-industrial complex and its role in the university community, but you would be wrong. I was only wondering if the lights were on in the bevatron, and how they looked. A physical fact.

I had trouble graduating from Berkeley, not because of this 5 inability to deal with ideas—I was majoring in English, and I could locate the house-and-garden imagery in "The Portrait of a Lady" as well as the next person, "imagery" being by definition the kind of specific that got my attention—but simply because I had neglected to take a course in Milton. For reasons which now sound baroque I needed a degree by the end of that summer, and the English department finally agreed, if I would come down from Sacramento every Friday and talk about the cosmology of "Paradise Lost," to certify me proficient in Milton. I did this. Some Fridays I took the Greyhound bus, other Fridays I caught

the Southern Pacific's City of San Francisco on the last leg of its
transcontinental trip. I can no longer tell you whether Milton put
the sun or the earth at the center of his universe in "Paradise
Lost," the central question of at least one century and a topic
about which I wrote 10,000 words that summer, but I can still
recall the exact rancidity of the butter in the City of San Francisco's
dining car, and the way the tinted windows on the Greyhound
bus cast the oil refineries around Carquinez Straits into a grayed
and obscurely sinister light. In short my attention was always
on the periphery, on what I could see and taste and touch, on
the butter, and the Greyhound bus. During those years I was
traveling on what I knew to be a very shaky passport, forged
papers: I knew that I was no legitimate resident in any world of
ideas. I knew I couldn't think. All I knew then was what I couldn't
do. All I knew was what I wasn't, and it took me some years to
discover what I was.

Which was a writer.   6

By which I mean not a "good" writer or a "bad" writer but   7
simply a writer, a person whose most absorbed and passionate
hours are spent arranging words on pieces of paper. Had my
credentials been in order I would never have become a writer.
Had I been blessed with even limited access to my own mind
there would have been no reason to write. I write entirely to
find out what I'm thinking, what I'm looking at, what I see and
what it means. What I want and what I fear. Why did the oil
refineries around Carquinez Straits seem sinister to me in the
summer of 1956? Why have the night lights in the bevatron
burned in my mind for twenty years? *What is going on in these
pictures in my mind?*

When I talk about pictures in my mind I am talking, quite 8
specifically, about images that shimmer around the edges. There
used to be an illustration in every elementary psychology book
showing a cat drawn by a patient in varying stages of
schizophrenia. This cat had a shimmer around it. You could see
the molecular structure breaking down at the very edges of the
cat: the cat became the background and the background the cat,
everything intereacting, exchanging ions. People on hallucinogens
describe the same perception of objects. I'm not a schizophrenic,
nor do I take hallucinogens, but certain images do shimmer for
me. Look hard enough, and you can't miss the shimmer. It's
there. You can't think too much about these pictures that
shimmer. You just lie low and let them develop. You stay quiet.

You don't talk to many people and you keep your nervous system from shorting out and you try to locate the cat in the shimmer, the grammar in the picture.

Just as I meant "shimmer" literally I mean "grammar"   9
literally. Grammar is a piano I play by ear, since I seem to have been out of school the year the rules were mentioned. All I know about grammar is its infinite power. To shift the structure of a sentence alters the meaning of that sentence, as definitely and inflexibly as the position of a camera alters the meaning of the object photographed. Many people know about camera angles now, but not so many know about sentences. The arrangement of the words matters, and the arrangement you want can be found in the picture in your mind. The picture dictates the arrangement. The picture dictates whether this will be a sentence with or without clauses, a sentence that ends hard or a dying-fall sentence, long or short, active or passive. The picture tells you how to arrange the words and the arrangement of the words tells you, or tells me, what's going on in the picture. *Nota bene*:

It tells you.   10

You don't tell it.   11

Let me show you what I mean by pictures in the mind. I   12
began "Play It as It Lays" just as I have begun each of my novels, with no notion of "character" or "plot" or even "incident." I had only two pictures in my mind, more about which later, and a technical intention, which was to write a novel so elliptical and fast that it would be over before you noticed it, a novel so fast that it would scarcely exist on the page at all. About the pictures: the first was of white space. Empty space. This was clearly the picture that dictated the narrative intention of the book—a book in which anything that happened would happen off the page, a "white" book to which the reader would have to bring his or her own bad dreams—and yet this picture told me no "story," suggested no situation. The second picture did. This second picture was of something actually witnessed. A young woman with long hair and a short white halter dress walks through the casino at the Riviera in Las Vegas at one in the morning. She crosses the casino alone and picks up a house telephone. I watch her because I have heard her paged, and recognize her name: she is a minor actress I see around Los Angeles from time to time, in places like Jax and once in a gynecologist's office in the Beverly Hills Clinic, but have never met. I know nothing about her. Who is paging her? Why is she here to be paged? How exactly did she

come to this? It was precisely this moment in Las Vegas that made "Play It as It Lays" begin to tell itself to me, but the moment appears in the novel only obliquely, in a chapter which begins:

"Maria made a list of things she would never do. She would 13 never: walk through the Sands or Caesar's alone after midnight. She would never: ball at a party, do S-M unless she wanted to, borrow furs from Abe Lipsey, deal. She would never: carry a Yorkshire in Beverly Hills."

That is the beginning of the chapter and that is also the end 14 of the chapter, which may suggest what I meant by "white space."

I recall having a number of pictures in my mind when I 15 began the novel I just finished, "A Book of Common Prayer." As a matter of fact one of these pictures was of that bevatron I mentioned, although I would be hard put to tell you a story in which nuclear energy figured. Another was a newspaper photograph of a hijacked 707 burning on the desert in the Middle East. Another was the night view from a room in which I once spent a week with paratyphoid, a hotel room on the Colombian coast. My husband and I seemed to be on the Colombian coast representing the United States of America at a film festival (I recall invoking the name "Jack Valenti" a lot, as if its reiteration could make me well), and it was a bad place to have fever, not only because my indisposition offended our hosts but because every night in this hotel the generator failed. The lights went out. The elevator stopped. My husband would go to the event of the evening and make excuses for me and I would stay alone in this hotel room, in the dark. I remember standing at the window trying to call Bogotá (the telephone seemed to work on the same principle as the generator) and watching the night wind come up and wondering what I was doing eleven degrees off the equator with a fever of 103. The view from that window definitely figures in "A Book of Common Prayer," as does the burning 707, and yet none of these pictures told me the story I needed.

The picture that did, the picture that shimmered and made 16 these other images coalesce, was the Panama airport at 6 A.M. I was in this airport only once, on a plane to Bogotá that stopped for an hour to refuel, but the way it looked that morning remained superimposed on everything I saw until the day I finished "A Book of Common Prayer." I lived in that airport for several years. I can still feel the hot air when I step off the plane, can see the heat already rising off the tarmac at 6 A.M. I can feel my skirt damp and wrinkled on my legs. I can feel the asphalt stick to my sandals. I remember the big tail of a Pan American plane floating motionless down at the end of the tarmac. I remember the sound of a slot machine in the waiting room. I could tell you that I remember a particular woman in the airport, an American woman, a *norteamericana*, a thin *norteamericana* about 40 who wore a big square emerald in lieu of a wedding ring, but there was no such woman there.

I put this woman in the airport later. I made this woman up, 17 just as I later made up a country to put the airport in, and a family to run the country. This woman in the airport is neither catching a plane nor meeting one. She is ordering tea in the airport coffee shop. In fact she is not simply "ordering" tea but insisting that the water be boiled, in front of her, for twenty minutes. Why is this woman in this airport? Why is she going nowhere, where has she been? Where did she get that big emerald? What derangement, or disassociation, makes her believe that her will to see the water boiled can possibly prevail?

"She had been going to one airport or another for four 18 months, one could see it, looking at the visas on her passport. All those airports where Charlotte Douglas's passport had been stamped would have looked alike. Sometimes the sign on the tower would say 'Bienvenidos' and sometimes the sign on the tower would say 'Bienvenue,' some places were wet and hot and others dry and hot, but at each of these airports the pastel concrete walls would rust and stain and the swamp off the runway would be littered with the fuselages of cannibalized Fairchild F-227's and the water would need boiling.

"I knew why Charlotte went to the airport even if Victor 19 did not.

"I knew about airports." 20

These lines appear about halfway through "A Book of 21 Common Prayer," but I wrote them during the second week I worked on the book, long before I had any idea where Charlotte Douglas had been or why she went to airports. Until I wrote these lines I had no character called "Victor" in mind: the necessity for mentioning a name, and the name "Victor," occurred to me as I wrote the sentence. *I knew why Charlotte went to the airport* sounded incomplete. *I knew why Charlotte went to the airport even if Victor did not* carried a little more narrative drive. Most important of all, until I wrote these lines I did not know who "I" was, who was telling the story. I had intended until that moment that the "I" be no more than the voice of the author, a 19th-century omniscient narrator.

But there it was: 22

"I knew why Charlotte went to the airport even if Victor   23 did not.

"I knew about airports."   24

This "I" was the voice of no author in my house. This "I"   25 was someone who not only knew why Charlotte went to the airport but also knew someone called "Victor." Who was Victor? Who was this narrator? Why was this narrator telling me this story? Let me tell you one thing about why writers write: had I known the answer to any of these questions I would never have needed to write a novel.

Annie Dillard

■ ■ ■

Living Like Weasels

Annie Dillard was born in Pittsburgh, Pennsylvania, in 1945 and received a MA from Hollins College in Virginia in 1968. From 1975 to 1985 she was an editor at *Harper's Magazine*; currently, she is the writer-in-residence at Wesleyan University in Middletown, Connecticut. Many distinctions have been awarded to her writing, including the Pulitzer Prize in 1975 for *Pilgrim at Tinker Creek,* a seminal work of non-fiction that depicts her walks in Virginia's Roanoke Valley and has often evoked critical comparison to Thoreau. She has received grants from the Guggenheim Foundation and the National Endowment for the Arts. She has published several books in various genres: poetry (*Mornings Like This,* 1995), fiction (*The Living,* 1982), and memoir (*An American Childhood,* 1987). Her most recent work is *For the Time Being* (1999). The following essay was first published in *Teaching a Stone To Talk: Expeditions and Encounters* (1982), a work the *Boston Globe* cited as one of the best books of the 80s. In this work she depicts, with incandescent detail, the wonders of the natural world.

A weasel is wild. Who knows what he thinks? He sleeps in his 1 underground den, his tail draped over his nose. Sometimes he lives in his den for two days without leaving. Outside, he stalks rabbits, mice, muskrats, and birds, killing more bodies than he can eat warm, and often dragging the carcasses home. Obedient to instinct, he bites his prey at the neck, either splitting the jugular vein at the throat or crunching the brain at the base of the skull, and he does not let go. One naturalist refused to kill a weasel who was socketed into his hand deeply as a rattlesnake. The man could in no way pry the tiny weasel off, and he had to walk half a mile to water, the weasel dangling from his palm, and soak him off like a stubborn label.

And once, says Ernest Thompson Seton—once, a man shot 2 an eagle out of the sky. He examined the eagle and found the dry skull of a weasel fixed by the jaws to his throat. The supposition is that the eagle had pounced on the weasel and the weasel swiveled and bit as instinct taught him, tooth to neck, and nearly

won. I would like to have seen that eagle from the air a few weeks
or months before he was shot: was the whole weasel still attached
to his feathered throat, a fur pendant? Or did the eagle eat what
he could reach, gutting the living weasel with his talons before
his breast, bending his beak, cleaning the beautiful airborne bones?

I have been reading about weasels because I saw one last week.   3
I startled a weasel who startled me, and we exchanged a long glance.

Twenty minutes from my house, through the woods by the   4
quarry and across the highway, is Hollins Pond, a remarkable
piece of shallowness, where I like to go at sunset and sit on a tree
trunk. Hollins Pond is also called Murray's Pond; it covers two
acres of bottomland near Tinker Creek with six inches of water
and six thousand lily pads. In winter, brown-and-white steers
stand in the middle of it, merely dampening their hooves; from
the distant shore they look like miracle itself, complete with
miracle's nonchalance. Now, in summer, the steers are gone. The
water lilies have blossomed and spread to a green horizontal
plane that is terra firma to plodding blackbirds, and tremulous
ceiling to black leeches, crayfish, and carp.

This is, mind you, suburbia. It is a five-minute walk in three   5
directions to rows of houses, though none is visible here. There's
a 55 mph highway at one end of the pond, and a nesting pair of
wood ducks at the other. Under every bush is a muskrat hole or
a beer can. The far end is an alternating series of fields and woods,
fields and woods, threaded everywhere with motorcycle tracks—
in whose bare clay wild turtles lay eggs.

So. I had crossed the highway, stepped over two low barbed-   6
wire fences, and traced the motorcycle path in all gratitude
through the wild rose and poison ivy of the pond's shoreline up
into high grassy fields. Then I cut down through the woods to
the mossy fallen tree where I sit. This tree is excellent. It makes a
dry, upholstered bench at the upper, marshy end of the pond, a
plush jetty raised from the thorny shore between a shallow blue
body of water and a deep blue body of sky.

The sun had just set. I was relaxed on the tree trunk,   7
ensconced in the lap of lichen, watching the lily pads at my feet
tremble and part dreamily over the thrusting path of a carp. A
yellow bird appeared to my right and flew behind me. It caught
my eye; I swiveled around—and the next instant, inexplicably, I
was looking down at a weasel, who was looking up at me.

Weasel! I'd never seen one wild before. He was ten inches   8
long, thin as a curve, a muscled ribbon, brown as fruitwood, soft-

furred, alert. His face was fierce, small and pointed as a lizard's; he would have made a good arrowhead. There was just a dot of chin, maybe two brown hairs' worth, and then the pure white fur began that spread down his underside. He had two black eyes I didn't see, any more than you see a window.

The weasel was stunned into stillness as he was emerging 9 from beneath an enormous shaggy wild rose bush four feet away. I was stunned into stillness twisted backward on the tree trunk. Our eyes locked, and someone threw away the key.

Our look was as if two lovers, or deadly enemies, met 10 unexpectedly on an overgrown path when each had been thinking of something else: a clearing blow to the gut. It was also a bright blow to the brain, or a sudden beating of brains, with all the charge and intimate grate of rubbed balloons. It emptied our lungs. It felled the forest, moved the fields, and drained the pond; the world dismantled and tumbled into that black hole of eyes. If you and I looked at each other that way, our skulls would split and drop to our shoulders. But we don't. We keep our skulls. So.

He disappeared. This was only last week, and already I don't 11 remember what shattered the enchantment. I think I blinked, I think I retrieved my brain from the weasel's brain and tried to memorize what I was seeing, and the weasel felt the yank of separation, the careening splash-down into real life and the urgent current of instinct. He vanished under the wild rose. I waited motionless, my mind suddenly full of data and my spirit with pleadings, but he didn't return.

Please do not tell me about "approach-avoidance conflicts." 12 I tell you I've been in that weasel's brain for sixty seconds, and he was in mine. Brains are private places, muttering through unique and secret tapes—but the weasel and I both plugged into another tape simultaneously, for a sweet and shocking time. Can I help it if it was a blank?

What goes on in his brain the rest of the time? What does a 13 weasel think about? He won't say. His journal is tracks in clay, a spray of feathers, mouse blood and bone: uncollected, unconnected, loose-leaf, and blown.

I would like to learn, or remember, how to live. I come to 14 Hollins Pond not so much to learn how to live as, frankly, to forget about it. That is, I don't think I can learn from a wild animal how to live in particular—shall I suck warm blood, hold my tail high, walk with my footprints precisely over the prints of my hands?— but I might learn something of mindlessness, something of the

purity of living in the physical senses and the dignity of living
without bias or motive. The weasel lives in necessity and we live
in choice, hating necessity and dying at the last ignobly in its talons.
I would like to live as I should, as the weasel lives as he should.
And I suspect that for me the way is like the weasel's: open to time
and death painlessly, noticing everything, remembering nothing,
choosing the given with a fierce and pointed will.

I missed my chance. I should have gone for the throat. I should   15
have lunged for that streak of white under the weasel's chin and
held on, held on through mud and into the wild rose, held on for a
dearer life. We could live under the wild rose as weasels, mute and
uncomprehending. I could very calmly go wild. I could live two
days in the den, curled, leaning on mouse fur, sniffing bird bones,
blinking, licking, breathing musk, my hair tangled in the roots of
grasses. Down is a good place to go, where the mind is single.
Down is out, out of your ever-loving mind and back to your careless
senses. I remember muteness as a prolonged and giddy fast, where
every moment is a feast of utterance received. Time and events are
merely poured, unremarked, and ingested directly, like blood
pulsed into my gut through a jugular vein. Could two live that
way? Could two live under the wild rose, and explore by the pond,
so that the smooth mind of each is as everywhere present to the
other, and as received and as unchallenged, as falling snow?
We could, you know. We can live any way we want. People   16
take vows of poverty, chastity, and obedience—even of silence—
by choice. The thing is to stalk your calling in a certain skilled
and supple way, to locate the most tender and live spot and plug
into that pulse. This is yielding, not fighting. A weasel doesn't
"attack" anything; a weasel lives as he's meant to, yielding at
every moment to the perfect freedom of single necessity.

I think it would be well, and proper, and obedient, and pure,   17
to grasp your one necessity and not let it go, to dangle from it
limp wherever it takes you. Then even death, where you're going
no matter how you live, cannot you part. Seize it and let it seize
you up aloft even, till your eyes burn out and drop; let your
musky flesh fall off in shreds, and let your very bones unhinge
and scatter, loosened over fields, over fields and woods, lightly,
thoughtless, from any height at all, from as high as eagles.

E. M. Forster

■ ■ ■

My Wood

Edward Morgan Forster (1879–1970), writer of novels, essays, short stories, and literary criticism, was born in London and graduated from King's College, Cambridge, in 1901. Publishing his first four novels, *Where Angels Fear To Tread* (1905), *The Longest Journey* (1907), *A Room with a View* (1908), and *Howards End* (1910) in rather rapid succession and to much acclaim, he became a celebrity and was active in the elite literary and cultural Bloomsbury group, counting as his friends Leonard and Virginia Woolf, Lytton Strachey, and John Maynard Keynes. With the publication of *A Passage to India* (1924), perhaps his most celebrated work, Forster's reputation as one of the twentieth-century's finest novelists was sealed, yet it remained his final novel until the posthumous publication of *Maurice* (1971). Forster remained an intellectual and academic force until he died; he was made an honorary fellow of King's College, Cambridge, in 1946 and received the Order of Merit in 1969. He continued to write in a variety of genres including biography, the short story, and the essay; and his treatise on fiction, *Aspects of the Novel* (1927), based on a series of lectures he gave at Cambridge, is still often quoted. Forster gathered together many of his essays into two miscellanies, *Two Cheers for Democracy* (1951), and *Abinger Harvest* (1936), in which "My Wood" appears. The essay was first published in *The New Leader* in October, 1926.

A few years ago I wrote a book which dealt in part with the dif- 1 ficulties of the English in India. Feeling that they would have had no difficulties in India themselves, the Americans read the book freely. The more they read it the better it made them feel, and a cheque to the author was the result. I bought a wood with the cheque. It is not a large wood—it contains scarcely any trees, and it is intersected, blast it, by a public footpath. Still, it is the first property that I have owned, so it is right that other people should participate in my shame, and should ask themselves, in accents that will vary in horror, this very important question: What is the effect of property upon the character? Don't let's touch economics; the effect of private ownership upon the community as a whole is another question—a more important question, perhaps, but another one. Let's keep to psychology. If you own things, what's their effect on you? What's the effect on me of my wood?

In the first place, it makes me feel heavy. Property does have 2 this effect. Property produces men of weight, and it was a man of weight who failed to get into the Kingdom of Heaven. He was not wicked, that unfortunate millionaire in the parable, he was only stout; he stuck out in front, not to mention behind, and as he wedged himself this way and that in the crystalline entrance and bruised his well-fed flanks, he saw beneath him a comparatively slim camel passing through the eye of a needle and being woven into the robe of God. The Gospels all through couple stoutness and slowness. They point out what is perfectly obvious, yet seldom realized: that if you have a lot of things you cannot move about a lot, that furniture requires dusting, dusters require servants, servants require insurance stamps, and the whole tangle of them makes you think twice before you accept an invitation to dinner or go for a bathe in the Jordan. Sometimes the Gospels proceed further and say with Tolstoy that property is sinful; they approach the difficult ground of asceticism here, where I cannot follow them. But as to the immediate effects of property on people, they just show straightforward logic. It produces men of weight. Men of weight cannot, by definition, move like the lightning from the East unto the West, and the ascent of a fourteen-stone bishop into a pulpit is thus the exact antithesis of the coming of the Son of Man. My wood makes me feel heavy.

In the second place, it makes me feel it ought to be larger.   3

The other day I heard a twig snap in it. I was annoyed at 4 first, for I thought that someone was blackberrying, and depreciating the value of the undergrowth. On coming nearer, I saw it was not a man who had trodden on the twig and snapped it, but a bird, and I felt pleased. My bird. The bird was not equally pleased. Ignoring the relation between us, it took fright as soon as it saw the shape of my face, and flew straight over the boundary hedge into a field, the property of Mrs. Henessy, where it sat down with a loud squawk. It had become Mrs. Henessy's bird. Something seemed grossly amiss here, something that would not have occurred had the wood been larger. I could not afford to buy Mrs. Henessy out, I dared not murder her, and limitations of this sort beset me on every side. Ahab did not want that vineyard—he only needed it to round off his property, preparatory to plotting a new curve—and all the land around my wood has become necessary to me in order to round off the wood. A boundary protects. But—poor little thing—the boundary ought in its turn to be protected. Noises on the edge of it. Children throw stones. A little more, and then a little more, until we reach the sea. Happy Canute! Happier Alexander! And after all, why should even the world be the limit of possession? A rocket containing a Union Jack, will, it is hoped, be shortly fired at the moon. Mars. Sirius. Beyond which . . . But these immensities ended by saddening me. I could not suppose that my wood was the destined nucleus of universal dominion—it is so very small and contains no mineral wealth beyond the blackberries. Nor was I comforted when Mrs. Henessy's bird took alarm for the second time and flew clean away from us all, under the belief that it belonged to itself.

In the third place, property makes its owner feel that he ought 5 to do something to it. Yet he isn't sure what. A restlessness comes over him, a vague sense that he has a personality to express— the same sense which, without any vagueness, leads the artist to an act of creation. Sometimes I think I will cut down such trees as remain in the wood, at other times I want to fill up the gaps between them with new trees. Both impulses are pretentious and empty. They are not honest movements towards money-making or beauty. They spring from a foolish desire to express myself and from an inability to enjoy what I have got. Creation, property, enjoyment form a sinister trinity in the human mind. Creation and enjoyment are both very very good, yet they are often unattainable without a material basis, and at such moments property pushes itself in as a substitute, saying, "Accept me instead — I'm good enough for all three." It is not enough. It is, as Shakespeare said of lust, "The expense of spirit in a waste of shame": it is "Before, a joy proposed; behind, a dream." Yet we don't know how to shun it. It is forced on us by our economic system as the alternative to starvation. It is also forced on us by an internal defect in the soul, by the feeling that in property may lie the germs of self-development and of exquisite or heroic deeds. Our life on earth is, and ought to be, material and carnal. But we have not yet learned to manage our materialism and carnality properly; they are still entangled with the desire for ownership, where (in the words of Dante) "Possession is one with loss."

And this brings us to our fourth and final point: the 6 blackberries.

Blackberries are not plentiful in this meagre grove, but they 7 are easily seen from the public footpath which traverses it, and all too easily gathered. Foxgloves, too—people will pull up the foxgloves, and ladies of an educational tendency even grub for toadstools to show them on the Monday in class. Other ladies, less educated, roll down the bracken in the arms of their gentlemen friends. There is paper, there are tins. Pray, does my wood belong to me or doesn't it? And, if it does, should I not own it best by allowing no one else to walk there? There is a wood near Lyme Regis, also cursed by a public footpath, where the owner has not hesitated on this point. He has built high stone walls each side of the path, and has spanned it by bridges, so that the public circulate like termites while he gorges on the blackberries unseen. He really does own his wood, this able chap. Dives in Hell did pretty well, but the gulf dividing him from Lazarus could be traversed by vision, and nothing traverses it here. And perhaps I shall come to this in time. I shall wall in and fence out until I really taste the sweets of property. Enormously stout, endlessly avaricious, pseudo-creative, intensely selfish, I shall weave upon my forehead the quadruple crown of possession until those nasty Bolshies come and take it off again and thrust me aside into the outer darkness.

Stephen Jay Gould

■■■

Sex, Drugs, Disasters, and the Extinction of Dinosaurs

Stephen Jay Gould (b. 1941), scientist and essayist, was born in New York City and holds a PhD in Paleontology (1967) from Columbia University. He is the Alexander Agassiz Professor of Zoology and Professor of Geology at Harvard University, and Curator of Invertebrate Paleontology at the Harvard Museum of Comparative Zoology. In 1974, Gould began writing "This View of Life," a column for *Natural History*, the monthly magazine of the American Museum of Natural History. This column, as well as essays appearing in other magazines such as *Discover* and *The New York Times*, has established him as a leading practitioner of the scientific essay. Many of these have been republished in his more than twenty books. He has received several prestigious awards and distinctions for his writing: the Science Book Prize in 1990 for *Wonderful Life: The Burgess Shale and the Nature of History* (1989); the National Book Critics' Award in 1982 for *The Mismeasure of Man;* and the Book Award for Science in 1981 for *The Panda's Thumb* (1980). He received a MacArthur Foundation prize fellowship in 1981. Gould has been praised for his contributions to science and to the public understanding of it, and is well-known for his opposition to the teaching of creationism alongside Darwinism. The following essay first appeared in *Discover* magazine in March 1984, and is reprinted from *The Flamingo's Smile: Reflections in Natural History* (1985).

Science, in its most fundamental definition, is a fruitful mode 1
of inquiry, not a list of enticing conclusions. The conclusions
are the consequence, not the essence.

My greatest unhappiness with most popular presentations 2
of science concerns their failure to separate fascinating claims
from the methods that scientists use to establish the facts
of nature. Journalists, and the public, thrive on controversial
and stunning statements. But science is, basically, a way of
knowing—in P. B. Medawar's apt words, "the art of the
soluble." If the growing corps of popular science writers would
focus on *how* scientists develop and defend those fascinating

claims, they would make their greatest possible contribution to public understanding.

Consider three ideas, proposed in perfect seriousness to 3 explain that greatest of all titillating puzzles—the extinction of dinosaurs. Since these three notions invoke the primally fascinating themes of our culture—sex, drugs, and violence— they surely reside in the category of fascinating claims. I want to show why two of them rank as silly speculation, while the other represents science at its grandest and most useful.

Science works with testable proposals. If, after much 4 compilation and scrutiny of data, new information continues to affirm a hypothesis, we may accept it provisionally and gain confidence as further evidence mounts. We can never be completely sure that a hypothesis is right, though we may be able to show with confidence that it is wrong. The best scientific hypotheses are also generous and expansive: they suggest extensions and implications that enlighten related, and even far distant, subjects. Simply consider how the idea of evolution has influenced virtually every intellectual field.

Useless speculation, on the other hand, is restrictive. It 5 generates no testable hypothesis, and offers no way to obtain potentially refuting evidence. Please note that I am not speaking of truth or falsity. The speculation may well be true; still, if it provides, in principle, no material for affirmation or rejection, we can make nothing of it. It must simply stand forever as an intriguing idea. Useless speculation turns in on itself and leads nowhere; good science, containing both seeds for its potential refutation and implications for more and different testable knowledge, reaches out. But, enough preaching. Let's move on to dinosaurs, and the three proposals for their extinction.

1. Sex: Testes function only in a narrow range of temperature (those of mammals hang externally in a scrotal sac because in ternal body temperatures are too high for their proper function). A worldwide rise in temperature at the close of the Cretaceous period caused the testes of dinosaurs to stop functioning and led to their extinction by sterilization of males.

2. Drugs: Angiosperms (flowering plants) first evolved toward the end of the dinosaurs' reign. Many of these plants contain psychoactive agents, avoided by mammals today as a result of their bitter taste. Dinosaurs had neither means to taste the bitterness nor livers effective enough to detoxify the substances. They died of massive overdoses.

3. Disasters: A large comet or asteroid struck the earth some 65 million years ago, lofting a cloud of dust into the sky and blocking sunlight, thereby suppressing photosynthesis and so drastically lowering world temperatures that dinosaurs and hosts of other creatures became extinct.

Before analyzing these three tantalizing statements, we must establish a basic ground rule often violated in proposals for the dinosaurs' demise. *There is no separate problem of the extinction of dinosaurs.* Too often we divorce specific events from their wider contexts and systems of cause and effect. The fundamental fact of dinosaur extinction is its synchrony with the demise of so many other groups across a wide range of habitats, from terrestrial to marine.

The history of life has been punctuated by brief episodes of 6 mass extinction. A recent analysis by University of Chicago paleontologists Jack Sepkoski and Dave Raup, based on the best and most exhaustive tabulation of data ever assembled, shows clearly that five episodes of mass dying stand well above the "background" extinctions of normal times (when we consider all mass extinctions, large and small, they seem to fall in a regular 26-million-year cycle[. . .]). The Cretaceous debacle, occurring 65 million years ago and separating the Mesozoic and Cenozoic eras of our geological time scale, ranks prominently among the five. Nearly all the marine plankton (single-celled floating creatures) died with geological suddenness; among marine invertebrates, nearly 15 percent of all families perished, including many previously dominant groups, especially the ammonites (relatives of squids in coiled shells). On land, the dinosaurs disappeared after more than 100 million years of unchallenged domination.

In this context, speculations limited to dinosaurs alone ignore 7 the larger phenomenon. We need a coordinated explanation for a system of events that includes the extinction of dinosaurs as one component. Thus it makes little sense, though it may fuel our desire to view mammals as inevitable inheritors of the earth, to guess that dinosaurs died because small mammals ate their eggs (a perennial favorite among untestable speculations). It seems most unlikely that some disaster peculiar to dinosaurs befell these massive beasts—and that the debacle happened to strike just when one of history's five great dyings had enveloped the earth for completely different reasons.

The testicular theory, an old favorite from the 1940s, had its 8 root in an interesting and thoroughly respectable study of temperature tolerances in the American alligator, published in the staid *Bulletin of the American Museum of Natural History* in 1946 by three experts on living and fossil reptiles—E. H. Colbert, my own first teacher in paleontology; R. B. Cowles; and C. M. Bogert.

The first sentence of their summary reveals a purpose beyond 9 alligators: "This report describes an attempt to infer the reactions of extinct reptiles, especially the dinosaurs, to high temperatures as based upon reactions observed in the modern alligator." They studied, by rectal thermometry, the body temperatures of alligators under changing conditions of heating and cooling. (Well, let's face it, you wouldn't want to try sticking a thermometer under a 'gator's tongue.) The predictions under test go way back to an old theory first stated by Galileo in the 1630s—the unequal scaling of surfaces and volumes. As an animal, or any object, grows (provided its shape doesn't change), surface areas must increase more slowly than volumes—since surfaces get larger as length squared, while volumes increase much more rapidly, as length cubed. Therefore, small animals have high ratios of surface to volume, while large animals cover themselves with relatively little surface.

Among cold-blooded animals lacking any physiological 10 mechanism for keeping their temperatures constant, small creatures have a hell of a time keeping warm—because they lose so much heat through their relatively large surfaces. On the other hand, large animals, with their relatively small surfaces, may lose heat so slowly that, once warm, they may maintain effectively constant temperatures against ordinary fluctuations of climate. (In fact, the resolution of the "hot-blooded dinosaur" controversy that burned so brightly a few years back may simply be that, while large dinosaurs possessed no physiological mechanism for constant temperature, and were not therefore warm-blooded in the technical sense, their large size and relatively small surface area kept them warm.)

Colbert, Cowles, and Bogert compared the warming rates of 11 small and large alligators. As predicted, the small fellows heated up (and cooled down) more quickly. When exposed to a warm sun, a tiny 50-gram (1.76-ounce) alligator heated up one degree Celsius every minute and a half, while a large alligator, 260 times bigger at 13,000 grams (28.7 pounds), took seven and a half minutes to gain a degree. Extrapolating up to an adult 10-ton dinosaur, they concluded that a one-degree rise in body temperature would take eighty-six hours. If large animals absorb heat so slowly (through their relatively small surfaces), they will also be unable to shed any excess heat gained when temperatures rise above a favorable level.

The authors then guessed that large dinosaurs lived at or 12 near their optimum temperatures; Cowles suggested that a rise in global temperatures just before the Cretaceous extinction caused the dinosaurs to heat up beyond their optimal tolerance—and, being so large, they couldn't shed the unwanted heat. (In a most unusual statement within a scientific paper, Colbert and Bogert then explicitly disavowed this speculative extension of their empirical work on alligators.) Cowles conceded that this excess heat probably wasn't enough to kill or even to enervate the great beasts, but since testes often function only within a narrow range of temperature, he proposed that this global rise might have sterilized all the males, causing extinction by natural contraception.

The overdose theory has recently been supported by UCLA 13 psychiatrist Ronald K. Siegel. Siegel has gathered, he claims, more than 2,000 records of animals who, when given access, administer various drugs to themselves—from a mere swig of alcohol to massive doses of the big H. Elephants will swill the equivalent of twenty beers at a time, but do not like alcohol in concentrations greater than 7 percent. In a silly bit of anthropocentric speculation, Siegel states that "elephants drink, perhaps, to forget . . . the anxiety produced by shrinking rangeland and the competition for food."

Since fertile imaginations can apply almost any hot idea to 14 the extinction of dinosaurs, Siegel found a way. Flowering plants did not evolve until late in the dinosaurs' reign. These plants also produced an array of aromatic, amino-acid-based alkaloids—the major group of psychoactive agents. Most mammals are "smart" enough to avoid these potential poisons. The alkaloids simply don't taste good (they are bitter); in any case, we mammals have livers happily supplied with the capacity to detoxify them. But, Siegel speculates, perhaps dinosaurs could neither taste the bitterness nor detoxify the substances once ingested. He recently told members of the American Psychological Association: "I'm not suggesting that all dinosaurs OD'd on plant drugs, but it certainly was a factor." He also argued that death by overdose may help explain why so many dinosaur fossils are found in contorted positions. (Do not go gentle into that good night.)

Extraterrestrial catastrophes have long pedigrees in the   15
popular literature of extinction, but the subject exploded again
in 1979, after a long lull, when the father-son, physicist-geologist
team of Luis and Walter Alvarez proposed that an asteroid,
some 10 km in diameter, struck the earth 65 million years ago
(comets, rather than asteroids, have since gained favor. [. . .]
Good science is self-corrective).

The force of such a collision would be immense, greater by far   16
than the megatonnage of all the world's nuclear weapons. . . . In
trying to reconstruct a scenario that would explain the
simultaneous dying of dinosaurs on land and so many creatures
in the sea, the Alvarezes proposed that a gigantic dust cloud,
generated by particles blown aloft in the impact, would so darken
the earth that photosynthesis would cease and temperatures drop
precipitously. (Rage, rage against the dying of the light.) The
single-celled photosynthetic oceanic plankton, with life cycles
measured in weeks, would perish outright, but land plants might
survive through the dormancy of their seeds (land plants were not
much affected by the Cretaceous extinction, and any adequate
theory must account for the curious pattern of differential
survival). Dinosaurs would die by starvation and freezing; small,
warm-blooded mammals, with more modest requirements for
food and better regulation of body temperature, would squeak
through. "Let the bastards freeze in the dark," as bumper stickers
of our chauvinistic neighbors in sunbelt states proclaimed several
years ago during the Northeast's winter oil crisis.

All three theories, testicular malfunction, psychoactive   17
overdosing, and asteroidal zapping, grab our attention mightily.
As pure phenomenology, they rank about equally high on any
hit parade of primal fascination. Yet one represents expansive
science, the others restrictive and untestable speculation. The
proper criterion lies in evidence and methodology; we must probe
behind the superficial fascination of particular claims.

How could we possibly decide whether the hypothesis of   18
testicular frying is right or wrong? We would have to know things
that the fossil record cannot provide. What temperatures were
optimal for dinosaurs? Could they avoid the absorption of excess
heat by staying in the shade, or in caves? At what temperatures
did their testicles cease to function? Were late Cretaceous climates
ever warm enough to drive the internal temperatures of dinosaurs
close to this ceiling? Testicles simply don't fossilize, and how
could we infer their temperature tolerances even if they did? In

short, Cowles's hypothesis is only an intriguing speculation leading nowhere. The most damning statement against it appeared right in the conclusion of Colbert, Cowles, and Bogert's paper, when they admitted: "It is difficult to advance any definite arguments against the hypothesis." My statement may seem paradoxical—isn't a hypothesis really good if you can't devise any arguments against it? Quite the contrary. It is simply untestable and unusable.

Siegel's overdosing has even less going for it. At least Cowles 19 extrapolated his conclusion from some good data on alligators. And he didn't completely violate the primary guideline of siting dinosaur extinction in the context of a general mass dying—for rise in temperature could be the root cause of a general catastrophe, zapping dinosaurs by testicular malfunction and different groups for other reasons. But Siegel's speculation cannot touch the extinction of ammonites or oceanic plankton (diatoms make their own food with good sweet sunlight; they don't OD on the chemicals of terrestrial plants). It is simply a gratuitous, attention-grabbing guess. It cannot be tested, for how can we know what dinosaurs tasted and what their livers could do? Livers don't fossilize any better than testicles.

The hypothesis doesn't even make any sense in its own 20 context. Angiosperms were in full flower ten million years before dinosaurs went the way of all flesh. Why did it take so long? As for the pains of a chemical death recorded in contortions of fossils, I regret to say (or rather I'm pleased to note for the dinosaurs' sake) that Siegel's knowledge of geology must be a bit deficient: muscles contract after death and geological strata rise and fall with motions of the earth's crust after burial—more than enough reason to distort a fossil's pristine appearance.

The impact story, on the other hand, has a sound basis in 21 evidence. It can be tested, extended, refined, and, if wrong, disproved. The Alvarezes did not just construct an arresting guess for public consumption. They proposed their hypothesis after laborious geochemical studies with Frank Asaro and Helen Michael had revealed a massive increase of iridium in rocks deposited right at the time of extinction. Iridium, a rare metal of the platinum group, is virtually absent from indigenous rocks of the earth's crust; most of our iridium arrives on extraterrestrial objects that strike the earth.

The Alvarez hypothesis bore immediate fruit. Based originally 22 on evidence from two European localities, it led geochemists throughout the world to examine other sediments of the same age. They found abnormally high amounts of iridium everywhere—from continental rocks of the western United States to deep sea cores from the South Atlantic.

Cowles proposed his testicular hypothesis in the mid-1940s. 23 Where has it gone since then? Absolutely nowhere, because scientists can do nothing with it. The hypothesis must stand as a curious appendage to a solid study of alligators. Siegel's overdose scenario will also win a few press notices and fade into oblivion. The Alvarezes' asteroid falls into a different category altogether, and much of the popular commentary has missed this essential distinction by focusing on the impact and its attendant results, and forgetting what really matters to a scientist—the iridium. If you talk just about asteroids, dust, and darkness, you tell stories no better and no more entertaining than fried testicles or terminal trips. It is the iridium—the source of testable evidence—that counts and forges the crucial distinction between speculation and science.

The proof, to twist a phrase, lies in the doing. Cowles's 24 hypothesis has generated nothing in thirty-five years. Since its proposal in 1979, the Alvarez hypothesis has spawned hundreds of studies, a major conference, and attendant publications. Geologists are fired up. They are looking for iridium at all other extinction boundaries. Every week exposes a new wrinkle in the scientific press. Further evidence that the Cretaceous iridium represents extraterrestrial impact and not indigenous volcanism continues to accumulate. As I revise this essay in November 1984 (this paragraph will be out of date when the book is published), new data include chemical "signatures" of other isotopes indicating unearthly provenance, glass spherules of a size and sort produced by impact and not by volcanic eruptions, and high-pressure varieties of silica formed (so far as we know) only under the tremendous shock of impact.

My point is simply this: Whatever the eventual outcome 25 (I suspect it will be positive), the Alvarez hypothesis is exciting, fruitful science because it generates tests, provides us with things to do, and expands outward. We are having fun, battling back and forth, moving toward a resolution, and extending the hypothesis beyond its original scope[. . . .]

As just one example of the unexpected, distant cross- 26 fertilization that good science engenders, the Alvarez hypothesis made a major contribution to a theme that has riveted public

attention in the past few months—so-called nuclear winter[. . .].
In a speech delivered in April 1982, Luis Alvarez calculated the
energy that a ten-kilometer asteroid would release on impact.
He compared such an explosion with a full nuclear exchange
and implied that all-out atomic war might unleash similar
consequences.

This theme of impact leading to massive dust clouds and 27
falling temperatures formed an important input to the decision
of Carl Sagan and a group of colleagues to model the climatic
consequences of nuclear holocaust. Full nuclear exchange would
probably generate the same kind of dust cloud and darkening
that may have wiped out the dinosaurs. Temperatures would
drop precipitously and agriculture might become impossible.
Avoidance of nuclear war is fundamentally an ethical and
political imperative, but we must know the factual consequences
to make firm judgments. I am heartened by a final link across
disciplines and deep concerns—another criterion, by the way, of
science at its best. A recognition of the very phenomenon that
made our evolution possible by exterminating the previously
dominant dinosaurs and clearing a way for the evolution of
large mammals, including us, might actually help to save us
from joining those magnificent beasts in contorted poses among
the strata of the earth.

Charles Lamb

■ ■ ■

from A Dissertation Upon Roast Pig

Charles Lamb (1775–1834), essayist and literary critic, is remembered for his distinguished friendships, his devotion to his mentally ill sister, his contributions to the Romantics' revived interest in Elizabethan drama and Shakespearean criticism, and for raising the art and profile of English prose writing. A friend to many of the leading writers of his day, among them Samuel Taylor Coleridge, William Hazlitt, and William Godwin, Lamb was eulogized in a poem by William Wordsworth as having a "genius [that] triumphed over seeming wrong . . . [and a] Humour and wild instinctive wit." Lamb was renowned for the sacrifice he made to care for his older sister Mary, who in 1796 in a moment of insanity stabbed their mother to death. Charles successfully petitioned to become her guardian, and together they wrote children's stories, including a well-known adaptation of Shakespeare for children. As an essayist, Lamb wrote under the pseudonym Elia, creating a persona whose style was idiosyncratic and humour self-deprecating. The following essay was first published in *The London Magazine* in September 1822, and later in a collection entitled *The Essays of Elia* (1823).

O f all the delicacies in the whole *mundus edibilis*,[1] I will maintain [roast pig] to be the most delicate—*princeps obsoniorum*.[2]   1

I speak not of your grown porkers—things between pig and pork—those hobbydehoys—but a young and tender suckling—under a moon old—guiltless as yet of the sty—with no original speck of the *amor immunditiæ*,[3] the hereditary failing of the first parent, yet manifest—his voice as yet not broken, but something between a childish treble, and a grumble—the mild forerunner, or *praeludium*,[4] of a grunt.   2

---

[1] edible world
[2] foremost of delicacies
[3] love of uncleanliness
[4] prelude

He must be roasted. I am not ignorant that our ancestors ate   3
them seethed, or boiled—but what a sacrifice of the exterior
tegument!

There is no flavour comparable, I will contend, to that of the   4
crisp, tawny, well-watched, not over-roasted, *crackling*, as it is
well called—the very teeth are invited to their share of the
pleasure at this banquet in overcoming the coy, brittle
resistance—with the adhesive oleaginous—O call it not fat—but
an indefinable sweetness growing up to it—the tender
blossoming of fat—fat cropped in the bud—taken in the shoot—
in the first innocence—the cream and quintessence of the child-
pig's yet pure food—the lean, no lean, but a kind of animal
manna—or, rather, fat and lean (if it must be so) so blended and
running into each other, that both together make but one
ambrosian result, or common substance.

Behold him, while he is doing—it seemeth rather a refreshing   5
warmth, than a scorching heat, that he is so passive to. How
equably he twirleth round the string!—Now he is just done. To
see the extreme sensibility of that tender age, he hath wept out his
pretty eyes—radiant jellies—shooting stars—

See him in the dish, his second cradle, how meek he lieth!—   6
wouldst thou have had this innocent grow up to the grossness
and indocility which too often accompany maturer swinehood?
Ten to one he would have proved a glutton, a sloven, an obstinate,
disagreeable animal—wallowing in all manner of filthy
conversation—from these sins he is happily snatched away—

> Ere sin could blight, or sorrow fade,
> Death came with timely care—

his memory is odoriferous—no clown curseth, while his stomach
half rejecteth, the rank bacon—no coalheaver bolteth him in
reeking sausages—he hath a fair sepulchre in the grateful stomach
of the judicious epicure—and for such a tomb might be content
to die.

He is the best of Sapors. Pine-apple is great. She is indeed   7
almost too transcendent—a delight, if not sinful, yet so like to
sinning, that really a tender-conscienced person would do well to
pause—too ravishing for mortal taste, she woundeth and
excoriateth the lips that approach her—like lovers' kisses, she
biteth—she is a pleasure bordering on pain from the fierceness
and insanity of her relish—but she stoppeth at the palate—she

meddleth not with the appetite—and the coarsest hunger might barter her consistently for a mutton chop.

Pig—let me speak his praise—is no less provocative of the   8
appetite, than he is satisfactory to the criticalness of the censorious palate. The strong man may batten on him, and the weakling refuseth not his mild juices.

Unlike to mankind's mixed characters, a bundle of virtues   9
and vices, inexplicably intertwisted, and not to be unravelled without hazard, he is—good throughout. No part of him is better or worse than another. He helpeth, as far as his little means extend, all around. He is the least envious of banquets. He is all neighbours' fare.

I am one of those, who freely and ungrudgingly impart a   10
share of the good things of this life which fall to their lot (few as mine are in this kind) to a friend. I protest I take as great an interest in my friend's pleasures, his relishes, and proper satisfactions, as in mine own. "Presents," I often say, "endear Absents." Hares, pheasants, partridges, snipes, barn-door chickens (those "tame villatic fowl"), capons, plovers, brawn, barrels of oysters, I dispense as freely as I receive them. I love to taste them, as it were, upon the tongue of my friend. But a stop must be put somewhere. One would not, like Lear, "give every thing." I make my stand upon pig. Methinks it is an ingratitude to the Giver of all good flavours, to extra-domiciliate, or send out of the house, slightingly, (under pretext of friendship, or I know not what) a blessing so particularly adapted, predestined, I may say, to my individual palate—It argues an insensibility.

I remember a touch of conscience in this kind at school. My   11
good old aunt, who never parted from me at the end of a holiday without stuffing a sweetmeat, or some nice thing, into my pocket, had dismissed me one evening with a smoking plum-cake, fresh from the oven. In my way to school (it was over London bridge) a grey-headed old beggar saluted me (I have no doubt at this time of day that he was a counterfeit). I had no pence to console him with, and in the vanity of self-denial, and the very coxcombry of charity, school-boy-like, I made him a present of— the whole cake! I walked on a little, buoyed up, as one is on such occasions, with a sweet soothing of self-satisfaction; but before I had got to the end of the bridge, my better feelings returned, and I burst into tears, thinking how ungrateful I had been to my good aunt, to go and give her good gift away to a stranger, that

I had never seen before, and who might be a bad man for aught I knew; and then I thought of the pleasure my aunt would be taking in thinking that I—I myself, and not another—would eat her nice cake—and what should I say to her the next time I saw her—how naughty I was to part with her pretty present—and the odour of that spicy cake came back upon my recollection, and the pleasure and the curiosity I had taken in seeing her make it, and her joy when she sent it to the oven, and how disappointed she would feel that I had never had a bit of it in my mouth at last—and I blamed my impertinent spirit of alms-giving, and out-of-place hypocrisy of goodness, and above all I wished never to see the face again of that insidious, good-for-nothing, old grey impostor.

Our ancestors were nice in their method of sacrificing these 12 tender victims. We read of pigs whipt to death with something of a shock, as we hear of any other obsolete custom. The age of discipline is gone by, or it would be curious to inquire (in a philosophical light merely) what effect this process might have towards intenerating and dulcifying a substance, naturally so mild and dulcet as the flesh of young pigs. It looks like refining a violet. Yet we should be cautious, while we condemn the inhumanity, how we censure the wisdom of the practice. It might impart a gusto—

I remember an hypothesis, argued upon by the young 13 students, when I was at St. Omer's, and maintained with much learning and pleasantry on both sides, "Whether, supposing that the flavour of a pig who obtained his death by whipping (*per flagellationem extremam*)[5] superadded a pleasure upon the palate of a man more intense than any possible suffering we can conceive in the animal, is man justified in using that method of putting the animal to death?" I forget the decision.

His sauce should be considered. Decidedly, a few bread 14 crums, done up with his liver and brains, and a dash of mild sage. But, banish, dear Mrs. Cook, I beseech you, the whole onion tribe. Barbecue your whole hogs to your palate, steep them in shalots, stuff them out with plantations of the rank and guilty garlic; you cannot poison them, or make them stronger than they are—but consider, he is a weakling—a flower.

---

[5] by means of extreme whipping

Margaret Laurence

■ ■ ■

Where the World Began

Margaret Laurence (1926–1987) was born in Neepawa, Manitoba. She received a BA from Winnipeg's United College (today the University of Winnipeg) in 1947, marrying that same year, and working after graduation for the *Winnipeg Citizen*. In 1949 she and her husband, a hydraulics engineer, moved to England and then to Somaliland and Ghana. Her first works, *A Tree for Poverty*, a translation of Somali folktales and poetry, and the short story "Uncertain Flowering," were written and published while she was in Africa, both in 1954; there, too, she set and drafted her first novel, *This Side Jordan*, written after she returned to Canada in 1957 and published in 1960. *The Tomorrow-Tamer* (1963) and *The Prophet's Camel Bell* (1963) are also products of her African experience. Separating from her husband in 1962, Laurence and her children moved to England, where she lived for ten years before resettling permanently in 1974 in southern Ontario. Between 1964 and 1974 she published her acclaimed Manawaka books, two of which, *A Jest of God* (1966) and *The Diviners* (1974), won the Governor-General's award for fiction. The others, also highly acclaimed, are *The Stone Angel* (1964), *The Fire Dwellers* (1969), and *A Bird in the House* (1970). One of Canada's most important writers, Laurence received many honorary degrees and was made a Companion of the Order of Canada in 1971. She was university writer-in-residence at Toronto, Western, and Trent, and served as Chancellor of Trent from 1981–1983. Laurence also wrote several children's stories and a number of occasional essays for a variety of periodicals and magazines, collected and published in 1976 as *Heart of a Stranger*. The following essay appears in this volume, and was first published in *Maclean's* magazine in December 1972.

■ _____ ■

[Laurence's Preface]
I wrote this article in 1971, when I was beginning my novel The Diviners. *I see now that I used it as one more means of working out a theme that appears in the novel, that is, the question of where one belongs and why, and the meaning to oneself of the ancestors, both the long-ago ones and those in remembered history. Until I re-read these articles, I didn't realize I had written so much on this theme before I ever dealt with it fictionally. I didn't realize, either, how compulsively I'd written about the river, the same river that appears in the novel.*

A strange place it was, that place where the world began. A   1
place of incredible happenings, splendours and revelations,
despairs like multitudinous pits of isolated hells. A place of
shadow-spookiness, inhabited by the unknowable dead. A place of
jubilation and of mourning, horrible and beautiful.

It was, in fact, a small prairie town.   2

Because that settlement and that land were my first and for   3
many years only real knowledge of this planet, in some profound
way they remain my world, my way of viewing. My eyes were
formed there. Towns like ours, set in a sea of land, have been
described thousands of times as dull, bleak, flat, uninteresting. I
have had it said to me that the railway trip across Canada is
spectacular, except for the prairies, when it would be desirable to
go to sleep for several days, until the ordeal is over. I am always
unable to argue this point effectively. All I can say is—well, you
really have to live there to know that country. The town of my
childhood could be called bizarre, agonizingly repressive or cruel
at times, and the land in which it grew could be called harsh in the
violence of its seasonal changes. But never merely flat or
uninteresting. Never dull.

In winter, we used to hitch rides on the back of the milk   4
sleigh, our moccasins squeaking and slithering on the hard rutted
snow of the roads, our hands in ice-bubbled mitts hanging onto
the box edge of the sleigh for dear life, while Bert grinned at us
through his great frosted moustache and shouted the horses into
speed, daring us to stay put. Those mornings, rising, there would
be the perpetual fascination of the frost feathers on windows,
the ferns and flowers and eerie faces traced there during the
night by unseen artists of the wind. Evenings, coming back from
skating, the sky would be black but not dark, for you could see
a cold glitter of stars from one side of the earth's rim to the other.
And then the sometime astonishment when you saw the
Northern Lights flaring across the sky, like the scrawled
signature of God. After a blizzard, when the snowploughs hadn't
yet got through, school would be closed for the day, the
assumption being that the town's young could not possibly
flounder through five feet of snow in the pursuit of education.
We would then gaily don snowshoes and flounder for miles out
into the white dazzling deserts, in pursuit of a different kind of
knowing. If you came back too close to night, through the woods
at the foot of the town hill, the thin black branches of poplar
and chokecherry now meringued with frost, sometimes you

heard coyotes. Or maybe the banshee wolf-voices were really only inside your head.

Summers were scorching, and when no rain came and the   5
wheat became bleached and dried before it headed, the faces of farmers and townsfolk would not smile much, and you took for granted, because it never seemed to have been any different, the frequent knocking at the back door and the young men standing there, mumbling or thrusting defiantly their request for a drink of water and a sandwich if you could spare it. They were riding the freights, and you never knew where they had come from, or where they might end up, if anywhere. The Drought and Depression were like evil deities which had been there always. You understood and did not understand.

Yet the outside world had its continuing marvels. The poplar   6
bluffs and the small river were filled and surrounded with a zillion different grasses, stones, and weed flowers. The meadowlarks sang undaunted from the twanging telephone wires along the gravel highway. Once we found an old flat-bottomed scow, and launched her, poling along the shallow brown waters, mending her with wodges of hastily chewed Spearmint, grounding her among the tangles of soft yellow marsh marigolds that grew succulently along the banks of the shrunken river, while the sun made our skins smell dusty-warm.

My best friend lived in an apartment above some stores on   7
Main Street (its real name was Mountain Avenue, goodness knows why), an elegant apartment with royal-blue velvet curtains. The back roof, scarcely sloping at all, was corrugated tin, of a furnace-like warmth on a July afternoon, and we would sit there drinking lemonade and looking across the back lane at the Fire Hall. Sometimes our vigil would be rewarded. Oh joy! Somebody's house burning down! We had an almost-perfect callousness in some ways. Then the wooden tower's bronze bell would clonk and toll like a thousand speeded funerals in a time of plague, and in a few minutes the team of giant black horses would cannon forth, pulling the fire wagon like some scarlet chariot of the Goths, while the firemen clung with one hand, adjusting their helmets as they went.

The oddities of the place were endless. An elderly lady used   8
to serve, as her afternoon tea offering to other ladies, soda biscuits spread with peanut butter and topped with a whole marshmallow. Some considered this slightly eccentric, when compared with chopped egg sandwiches, and admittedly talked

about her behind her back, but no one ever refused these delicacies or indicated to her that they thought she had slipped a cog. Another lady dyed her hair a bright and cheery orange, by strangers often mistaken at twenty paces for a feather hat. My own beloved stepmother wore a silver fox neckpiece, a whole pelt, *with the embalmed (?) head still on.* My Ontario Irish grandfather said, "sparrow grass," a more interesting term than asparagus. The town dump was known as "the nuisance grounds," a phrase fraught with weird connotations, as though the effluvia of our lives was beneath contempt but at the same time was subtly threatening to the determined and sometimes hysterical propriety of our ways.

Some oddities were, as idiom had it, "funny ha ha"; others   9
were "funny peculiar." Some were not so very funny at all. An old man lived, deranged, in a shack in the valley. Perhaps he wasn't even all that old, but to us he seemed a wild Methuselah figure, shambling among the underbrush and the tall couchgrass, muttering indecipherable curses or blessings, a prophet who had forgotten his prophesies. Everyone in town knew him, but no one knew him. He lived among us as though only occasionally and momentarily visible. The kids called him Andy Gump, and feared him. Some sought to prove their bravery by tormenting him. They were the mediaeval bear baiters, and he the lumbering bewildered bear, half blind, only rarely turning to snarl. Everything is to be found in a town like mine. Belsen, writ small but with the same ink.

All of us cast stones in one shape or another. In grade school,   10
among the vulnerable and violet girls we were, the feared and despised were those few older girls from what was charmingly termed "the wrong side of the tracks." Tough in talk and tougher in muscle, they were said to be whores already. And may have been, that being about the only profession readily available to them.

The dead lived in that place, too. Not only the grandparents   11
who had, in local parlance, "passed on" and who gloomed, bearded or bonneted, from the sepia photographs in old albums, but also the uncles, forever eighteen or nineteen, whose names were carved on the granite family stones in the cemetery, but whose bones lay in France. My own young mother lay in that graveyard, beside other dead of our kin, and when I was ten, my father, too, only forty, left the living town for the dead dwelling on the hill.

When I was eighteen, I couldn't wait to get out of that town, 12
away from the prairies. I did not know then that I would carry the
land and town all my life within my skull, that they would form
the mainspring and source of the writing I was to do, wherever
and however far away I might live.

This was my territory in the time of my youth, and in a sense 13
my life since then has been an attempt to look at it, to come to
terms with it. Stultifying to the mind it certainly could be, and
sometimes was, but not to the imagination. It was many things,
but it was never dull.

The same, I now see, could be said for Canada in general. 14
Why on earth did generations of Canadians pretend to believe
this country dull? We knew perfectly well it wasn't. Yet for so
long we did not proclaim what we knew. If our upsurge of so-
called nationalism seems odd or irrelevant to outsiders, and
even to some of our own people (*what's all the fuss about?*), they
might try to understand that for many years we valued
ourselves insufficiently, living as we did under the huge
shadows of those two dominating figures, Uncle Sam and
Britannia. We have only just begun to value ourselves, our land,
our abilities. We have only just begun to recognize our legends
and to give shape to our myths.

There are, God knows, enough aspects to deplore about this 15
country. When I see the killing of our lakes and rivers with
industrial wastes, I feel rage and despair. When I see our
industries and natural resources increasingly taken over by
America, I feel an overwhelming discouragement, especially as I
cannot simply say "damn Yankees." It should never be forgotten
that it is we ourselves who have sold such a large amount of our
birthright for a mess of plastic Progress. When I saw the War
Measures Act being invoked in 1970, I lost forever the vestigial
remains of the naive wish-belief that repression could not happen
here, or would not. And yet, of course, I had known all along in
the deepest and often hidden caves of the heart that anything
can happen anywhere, for the seed of both man's freedom and his
captivity are found everywhere, even in the microcosm of a
prairie town. But in raging against our injustices, our stupidities,
I do so *as family*, as I did, and still do in writing, about those
aspects of my town which I hated and which are always in some
ways aspects of myself.

The land still draws me more than other lands. I have lived 16
in Africa and in England, but splendid as both can be, they do

not have the power to move me in the same way as, for example, that part of southern Ontario where I spent four months last summer in a cedar cabin beside a river. "Scratch a Canadian, and you find a phony pioneer," I used to say to myself in warning. But all the same it is true, I think, that we are not yet totally alienated from physical earth, and let us only pray we do not become so. I once thought that my lifelong fear and mistrust of cities made me a kind of old-fashioned freak; now I see it differently.

The cabin has a long window across its front western wall, 17 and sitting at the oak table there in the mornings, I used to look out at the river and at the tall trees beyond, green-gold in the early light. The river was bronze; the sun caught it strangely, reflecting upon its surface the near-shore sand ripples underneath. Suddenly, the crescenting of a fish, gone before the eye could clearly give image to it. The old man next door said these leaping fish were carp. Himself, he preferred muskie, for he was a real fisherman and the muskie gave him a fight. The wind most often blew from the south, and the river flowed toward the south, so when the water was wind-riffled, and the current was strong, the river seemed to be flowing both ways. I liked this, and interpreted it as an omen, a natural symbol.

A few years ago, when I was back in Winnipeg, I gave a talk 18 at my old college. It was open to the public, and afterward a very old man came up to me and asked me if my maiden name had been Wemyss. I said yes, thinking he might have known my father or my grandfather. But no. "When I was a young lad," he said, "I once worked for your great-grandfather, Robert Wemyss, when he had the sheep ranch at Raeburn." I think that was a moment when I realized all over again something of great importance to me. My long-ago families came from Scotland and Ireland, but in a sense that no longer mattered so much. My true roots were here.

I am not very patriotic, in the usual meaning of that word. I 19 cannot say "My country right or wrong" in any political, social or literary context. But one thing is inalterable, for better or worse, for life.

This is where my world began. A world which includes the 20 ancestors—both my own and other people's ancestors who became mine. A world which formed me, and continues to do so, even while I fought it in some of its aspects, and continue to do so. A world which gave me my own lifework to do, because it was here that I learned the sight of my own particular eyes.

Stephen Leacock

■ ■ ■

Roughing It in the Bush: My Plans for Moose Hunting in the Canadian Wilderness

Stephen Leacock (1869–1944), economist, essayist, historian, and humorist, was born in Swanmore, Hampshire, England, and was six when his family moved to Canada. Despite financial hardship, brought on by his father's deserting the family, Leacock received a BA from the University of Toronto in 1891 and a PhD from the University of Chicago in 1903. He was the head of the Department of Economics and Political Science at McGill University from 1908 to 1936. His first book, *Elements of Political Science* (1906), became the standard text of the discipline for many years, and he went on to author more than sixty books, academic and humorous, fiction and non-fiction. His first humorous book, *Literary Lapses* (1910), was immediately successful, and he followed it with *Nonsense Novels* (1911), thereafter writing a total of twenty-five humorous books, including the comic masterpieces *Sunshine Sketches of a Little Town* (1912) and *Arcadian Adventures with the Idle Rich* (1914). Between 1915 and 1925, Leacock was the world's best-known English humorist. Leacock's humour, though it may not always have conformed to his credo that humour must be "kindly," has been characterized as typically Canadian, and he received numerous honorary degrees and distinctions during his lifetime, including the Governor-General's award. Since 1947 the Stephen Leacock Medal for Humour has been awarded to the best humorous book written by a Canadian author. The following selection comes from *Over the Footlights and Other Fancies* (1923), a collection of typically Leacockian essays and sketches.

The season is now opening when all those who have a manly 1 streak in them like to get out into the bush and "rough it" for a week or two of hunting and fishing. For myself, I never feel that the autumn has been well spent unless I can get out after the moose. And when I go I like to go right into the bush and "rough it"—get clear away from civilization, out in the open, and take fatigue or hardship just as it comes.

So this year I am making all my plans to get away for a couple 2
of weeks of moose hunting along with my brother George and my
friend Tom Gass. We generally go together because we are all of
us men who like the rough stuff and are tough enough to stand
the hardship of living in the open. The place we go to is right in
the heart of the primitive Canadian forest, among big timber,
broken with lakes as still as glass, just the very ground for moose.

We have a kind of lodge up there. It's just a rough place that 3
we put up, the three of us, the year before last,—built out of
tamarack logs faced with a broad axe. The flies, while we were
building it, were something awful. Two of the men that we sent
in there to build it were so badly bitten that we had to bring them
out a hundred miles to a hospital. None of us saw the place while
we were building it,—we were all busy at the time,—but the
teamsters who took in our stuff said it was the worst season for
the black flies that they ever remembered.

Still we hung to it, in spite of the flies, and stuck at it till we 4
got it built. It is, as I say, only a plain place but good enough to
rough it in. We have one big room with a stone fireplace, and
bedrooms round the sides, with a wide verandah, properly
screened, all along the front. The verandah has a row of upright
tamaracks for its posts and doesn't look altogether bad. In the
back part we have quarters where our man sleeps. We had an
ice-house knocked up while they were building and water laid on
in pipes from a stream. So that on the whole the place has a kind
of rough comfort about it,—good enough anyway for fellows
hunting moose all day.

The place, nowadays, is not hard to get at. The government 5
has just built a colonization highway, quite all right for motors,
that happens to go within a hundred yards of our lodge.

We can get the railway for a hundred miles, and then the 6
highway for forty, and the last hundred yards we can walk. But
this season we are going to cut out the railway and go the whole
way from the city in George's car with our kit with us.

George has one of those great big cars with a roof and thick 7
glass sides. Personally none of the three of us would have
preferred to ride in a luxurious darned thing like that. Tom says
that as far as he is concerned he'd much sooner go into the bush
over a rough trail in a buckboard, and for my own part a team of
oxen would be more the kind of thing that I'd wish.

However the car is there, so we might as well use the thing especially as the provincial government has built the fool highway right into the wilderness. By taking the big car also we can not only carry all the hunting outfit that we need but we can also, if we like, shove in a couple of small trunks with a few clothes. This may be necessary as it seems that somebody has gone and slapped a great big frame hotel right there in the wilderness, not half a mile from the place we go to. The hotel we find a regular nuisance. It gave us the advantage of electric light for our lodge (a thing none of us care about), but it means more fuss about clothes. Clothes, of course, don't really matter when a fellow is roughing it in the bush, but Tom says that we might find it necessary to go over to the hotel in the evenings to borrow coal oil or a side of bacon or any rough stuff that we need; and they do such a lot of dressing up at these fool hotels now that if we do go over for bacon or anything in the evening we might just as well slip on our evening clothes, as we could chuck them off the minute we get back. George thinks it might not be a bad idea,— just as a way of saving all our energy for getting after the moose,—to dine each evening at the hotel itself. He knew some men who did that last year and they told him that the time saved for moose hunting in that way is extraordinary. George's idea is that we could come in each night with our moose,—such and such a number as the case might be—either bringing them with us or burying them where they die,—change our things, slide over to the hotel and get dinner and then beat it back into the bush by moonlight and fetch in the moose. It seems they have a regular two dollar table d'hôte dinner at the hotel,—just rough stuff of course but after all, as we all admit, we don't propose to go out into the wilds to pamper ourselves with high feeding: a plain hotel meal in a home-like style at two dollars a plate is better than cooking up a lot of rich stuff over a camp fire.

If we *do* dine at the hotel we could take our choice each 9 evening between going back into the bush by moonlight to fetch in the dead moose from the different caches where we had hidden them, or sticking round the hotel itself for a while. It seems that there is dancing there. Nowadays such a lot of women and girls get the open air craze for the life in the bush that these big wilderness hotels are crowded with them. There is something about living in the open that attracts modern women and they like to get right away from everybody and everything; and of course hotels of this type in the open are nowadays always well closed in with screens so that there are no flies or anything of that sort.

So it seems that there is dancing at the hotel every evening,— nothing on a large scale or pretentious,—just an ordinary hardwood floor,—they may wax it a little for all I know,—and some sort of plain, rough Italian orchestra that they fetch up from the city. Not that any of us care for dancing. It's a thing that personally we wouldn't bother with. But it happens that there are a couple of young girls that Tom knows that are going to be staying at the hotel and of course naturally he wants to give them a good time. They are only eighteen and twenty (sisters) and that's really younger than we care for, but with young girls like that,—practically kids,—any man wants to give them a good time. So Tom says, and I think quite rightly, that as the kids are going to be there we may as well put in an appearance at the hotel and see that they are having a good time. Their mother is going to be with them too, and of course we want to give her a good time as well; in fact I think I will lend her my moose rifle and let her go out and shoot a moose. One thing we are all agreed upon in the arrangement of our hunting trip, is in not taking along anything to drink. Drinking spoils a trip of that sort. We all remember how in the old days we'd go out into a camp in the bush (I mean before there used to be any highway or any hotel) and carry in rye whiskey in demijohns (two dollars a gallon it was) and sit around the camp fire drinking it in the evenings. 10

But there's nothing in it. We all agree that the law being what it is, it is better to stick to it. It makes a fellow feel better. So we shall carry nothing in. I don't say that one might not have a flask or something in one's pocket in the car; but only as a precaution against accident or cold. And when we get to our lodge we all feel that we are a darned sight better without it. If we *should* need anything,—though it isn't likely,—there are still three cases of old Scotch whiskey, kicking around the lodge somewhere; I think they are kicking round in a little cement cellar with a locked door that we had made so as to use it for butter or anything of that sort. Anyway there are three, possibly four, or maybe, five, cases of Scotch there and if we should for any reason want it, there it is. But we are hardly likely to touch it,—unless we hit a cold snap, or a wet spell; —then we might; or if we strike hot dry weather. Tom says he thinks there are a couple of cases of champagne still in the cellar; some stuff that one of us must have shot in there just before prohibition came in. But we'll hardly use it. When a 11 man is out moose hunting from dawn to dusk he hasn't much use for champagne, not till he gets home anyway. The only thing that Tom says the champagne might come in useful for would be if we cared to ask the two kids over to some sort of dinner; it would be just a rough kind of camp dinner (we could hardly ask their mother to it) but we think we could manage it. The man we keep there used to be a butler in England, or something of the sort, and he could manage some kind of rough meal where the champagne might fit in.

There's only one trouble about our plans for our fall camp 12 that bothers us just a little. The moose are getting damn scarce about that place. There used, so they say, to be any quantity of them. There's an old settler up there that our man buys all our cream from who says that he remembers when the moose were so thick that they would come up and drink whiskey out of his dipper. But somehow they seem to have quit the place. Last year we sent our man out again and again looking for them and he never saw any. Three years ago a boy that works at the hotel said he saw a moose in the cow pasture back of the hotel and there were the tracks of a moose seen last year at the place not ten miles from the hotel where it had come to drink. But apart from these two exceptions the moose hunting has been poor.

Still, what does it matter? What we want is the *life*, the rough 13 life just as I have described it. If any moose comes to our lodge we'll shoot him, or tell the butler to. But if not,—well, we've got along without for ten years, I don't suppose we shall worry.

John Stuart Mill

■■■

from Of the Liberty of Thought and Discussion

Endowed with a capacious, inquiring mind, John Stuart Mill (1806–1873) contributed to many fields of nineteenth-century discourse. Born in London, he was an eminent philosopher, economist, logician, and ethical theorist who published works on a variety of topics and issues, including, for example, *A System of Logic (1843), Principles of Political Economy* (1848), and *The Subjection of Women* (1869). A child prodigy, Mill was strictly educated at home under the assiduous tutelage of his father, British historian and philosopher James Mill. Mastering classical Greek by the age of eight, he studied writers such as Herodotus and Isocrates, and by twelve was mastering subjects such as political economy and scholastic logic. The following selection is an excerpt from *On Liberty* (1859), a book that has created controversy since its publication. Its influence is comparable only to that of the *Communist Manifesto*, also published in the nineteenth century. In *On Liberty* Mill attempts to illustrate, as he states in his preface, "The nature and limits of power which can be legitimately exercised by society over the individual." This selection is the first part of Chapter Two, "Of the Liberty of Thought and Discussion," which presents the classical liberal argument that defends an individual's right to think freely, to seek the truth without repercussions, and to develop as an individual free from social restraint.

The time, it is to be hoped, is gone by, when any defence would   1
be necessary of the "liberty of the press" as one of the securities against corrupt or tyrannical government. No argument, we may suppose, can now be needed, against permitting a legislature or an executive, not identified in interest with the people, to prescribe opinions to them, and determine what doctrines or what arguments they shall be allowed to hear. This aspect of the question, besides, has been so often and so triumphantly enforced by preceding writers, that it needs not be specially insisted on in this place. Though the law of England, on the subject of the press, is as servile to this day as it was in the time of the Tudors, there is little

danger of its being actually put in force against political discussion, except during some temporary panic, when fear of insurrection drives ministers and judges from their propriety;[1] and, speaking generally, it is not, in constitutional countries, to be apprehended, that the government, whether completely responsible to the people or not, will often attempt to control the expression of opinion, except when in doing so it makes itself the organ of the general intolerance of the public. Let us suppose, therefore, that the government is entirely at one with the people, and never thinks of exerting any power of coercion unless in agreement with what it conceives to be their voice. But I deny the right of the people to exercise such coercion, either by themselves or by their government. The power itself is illegitimate. The best government has no more title to it than the worst. It is as noxious, or more noxious, when exerted in accordance with public opinion, than when in opposition to it. If all mankind minus one, were of one opinion, and only one person were of the contrary opinion, mankind would be no more justified in silencing that one person, than he, if he had the power, would be justified in silencing mankind. Were an opinion a personal possession of no value except to the owner; if to be obstructed in the enjoyment of it were simply a private injury, it would make some difference whether the injury was inflicted only on a few persons or on many. But the peculiar evil of silencing the expression of an opinion is, that it is robbing the human race; posterity as well as the existing generation; those who dissent from the opinion, still more than those who hold it. If the

---

[1] [Mill's note] These words had scarcely been written, when, as if to give them an emphatic contradiction, occurred the Government Press Prosecutions of 1858. That ill-judged interference with the liberty of public discussion has not, however, induced me to alter a single word in the text, nor has it at all weakened my conviction that, moments of panic excepted, the era of pains and penalties for political discussion has, in our own country, passed away. For, in the first place, the prosecutions were not persisted in; and, in the second, they were never, properly speaking, political prosecutions. The offence charged was not that of criticizing institutions, or the acts or persons of rulers, but of circulating what was deemed an immoral doctrine, the lawfulness of Tyrannicide.

If the arguments of the present chapter are of any validity, there ought to exist the fullest liberty of professing and discussing, as a matter of ethical conviction, any doctrine, however immoral it may be considered. It would, therefore, be irrelevant and out of place to examine here, whether the doctrine of Tyrannicide deserves that title. I shall content myself with saying that the subject has been at all times one of the open questions of morals: that the act of a private citizen in striking down a criminal, who, by raising himself above the law, has placed himself beyond the reach of legal punishment or control, has been accounted by whole nations, and by some of the best and wisest of men, not a crime, but an act of exalted virtue; and that, right or wrong, it is not of the nature of assassination, but of civil war. As such, I hold that the instigation to it, in a specific case, may be a proper subject of punishment, but only if an overt act has followed, and at least a probable connexion can be established between the act and the instigation. Even then, it is not a foreign government, but the very government assailed, which alone, in the exercise of self-defence, can legitimately punish attacks directed against its own existence.

opinion is right, they are deprived of the opportunity of exchanging error for truth: if wrong, they lose, what is almost as great a benefit, the clearer perception and livelier impression of truth, produced by its collision with error.

It is necessary to consider separately these two hypotheses, 2 each of which has a distinct branch of the argument corresponding to it. We can never be sure that the opinion we are endeavouring to stifle is a false opinion; and if we were sure, stifling it would be an evil still.

First: the opinion which it is attempted to suppress by 3 authority may possibly be true. Those who desire to suppress it, of course deny its truth; but they are not infallible. They have no authority to decide the question for all mankind, and exclude every other person from the means of judging. To refuse a hearing to an opinion, because they are sure that it is false, is to assume that *their* certainty is the same thing as *absolute* certainty. All silencing of discussion is an assumption of infallibility. Its condemnation may be allowed to rest on this common argument, not the worse for being common.

Unfortunately for the good sense of mankind, the fact of 4 their fallibility is far from carrying the weight in their practical judgement, which is always allowed to it in theory; for while every one well knows himself to be fallible, few think it necessary to take any precautions against their own fallibility, or admit the supposition that any opinion, of which they feel very certain, may be one of the examples of the error to which they acknowledge themselves to be liable. Absolute princes, or others who are accustomed to unlimited deference, usually feel this complete confidence in their own opinions on nearly all subjects. People more happily situated, who sometimes hear their opinions disputed, and are not wholly unused to be set right when they are wrong, place the same unbounded reliance only on such of their opinions as are shared by all who surround them, or to whom they habitually defer: for in proportion to a man's want of confidence in his own solitary judgement, does he usually repose, with implicit trust, on the infallibility of "the world" in general. And the world, to each individual, means the part of it with which he comes in contact; his party, his sect, his church, his class of society: the man may be called, by comparison, almost liberal and large-minded to whom it means anything so comprehensive as his own country or his own age. Nor is his

faith in this collective authority at all shaken by his being aware
that other ages, countries, sects, churches, classes, and parties
have thought, and even now think, the exact reverse. He
devolves upon his own world the responsibility of being in the
right against the dissentient worlds of other people; and it never
troubles him that mere accident has decided which of these
numerous worlds is the object of his reliance, and that the same
causes which make him a Churchman in London, would have
made him a Buddhist or a Confucian in Pekin. Yet it is as evident
in itself, as any amount of argument can make it, that ages are no
more infallible than individuals; every age having held many
opinions which subsequent ages have deemed not only false but
absurd; and it is as certain that many opinions, now general,
will be rejected by future ages, as it is that many, once general,
are rejected by the present.

The objection likely to be made to this argument would   5
probably take some such form as the following. There is no
greater assumption of infallibility in forbidding the propagation
of error, than in any other thing which is done by public authority
on its own judgement and responsibility. Judgement is given to
men that they may use it. Because it may be used erroneously, are
men to be told that they ought not to use it at all? To prohibit
what they think pernicious, is not claiming exemption from error,
but fulfilling the duty incumbent on them, although fallible, of
acting on their conscientious conviction. If we were never to act
on our opinions, because those opinions may be wrong, we
should leave all our interests uncared for, and all our duties
unperformed. An objection which applies to all conduct, can be
no valid objection to any conduct in particular. It is the duty of
governments, and of individuals, to form the truest opinions they
can; to form them carefully, and never impose them upon others
unless they are quite sure of being right. But when they are sure
(such reasoners may say), it is not conscientiousness but
cowardice to shrink from acting on their opinions, and allow
doctrines which they honestly think dangerous to the welfare of
mankind, either in this life or in another, to be scattered abroad
without restraint, because other people, in less enlightened times,
have persecuted opinions now believed to be true. Let us take
care, it may be said, not to make the same mistake: but
governments and nations have made mistakes in other things,
which are not denied to be fit subjects for the exercise of authority:
they have laid on bad taxes, made unjust wars. Ought we

therefore to lay on no taxes, and, under whatever provocation, make no wars? Men, and governments, must act to the best of their ability. There is no such thing as absolute certainty, but there is assurance sufficient for the purposes of human life. We may, and must, assume our opinion to be true for the guidance of our own conduct: and it is assuming no more when we forbid bad men to pervert society by the propagation of opinions which we regard as false and pernicious.

I answer, that it is assuming very much more. There is the 6 greatest difference between presuming an opinion to be true, because, with every opportunity for contesting it, it has not been refuted, and assuming its truth for the purpose of not permitting its refutation. Complete liberty of contradicting and disproving our opinion, is the very condition which justifies us in assuming its truth for purposes of action; and on no other terms can a being with human faculties have any rational assurance of being right.

When we consider either the history of opinion, or the 7 ordinary conduct of human life, to what is it to be ascribed that the one and the other are no worse than they are? Not certainly to the inherent force of the human understanding; for, on any matter not self-evident, there are ninety-nine persons totally incapable of judging of it, for one who is capable; and the capacity of the hundredth person is only comparative; for the majority of the eminent men of every past generation held many opinions now known to be erroneous, and did or approved numerous things which no one will now justify. Why is it, then, that there is on the whole a preponderance among mankind of rational opinions and rational conduct? If there really is this preponderance—which there must be, unless human affairs are, and have always been, in an almost desperate state—it is owing to a quality of the human mind, the source of everything respectable in man, either as an intellectual or as a moral being, namely, that his errors are corrigible. He is capable of rectifying his mistakes by discussion and experience. Not by experience alone. There must be discussion, to show how experience is to be interpreted. Wrong opinions and practices gradually yield to fact and argument: but facts and arguments, to produce any effect on the mind, must be brought before it. Very few facts are able to tell their own story, without comments to bring out their meaning. The whole strength and value, then, of human judgement, depending on the one property, that it can be set right when it is wrong, reliance can be placed on it only when the

means of setting it right are kept constantly at hand. In the case
of any person whose judgement is really deserving of confidence,
how has it become so? Because he has kept his mind open to
criticism of his opinions and conduct. Because it has been his
practice to listen to all that could be said against him; to profit by
as much of it as was just, and expound to himself, and upon
occasion to others, the fallacy of what was fallacious. Because
he has felt, that the only way in which a human being can make
some approach to knowing the whole of a subject, is by hearing
what can be said about it by persons of every variety of opinion,
and studying all modes in which it can be looked at by every
character of mind. No wise man ever acquired his wisdom in
any mode but this; nor is it in the nature of human intellect to
become wise in any other manner. The steady habit of correcting
and completing his own opinion by collating it with those of
others, so far from causing doubt and hesitation in carrying it
into practice, is the only stable foundation for a just reliance on
it: for, being cognisant of all that can, at least obviously, be said
against him, and having taken up his position against all
gainsayers—knowing that he has sought for objections and
difficulties, instead of avoiding them, and has shut out no light
which can be thrown upon the subject from any quarter—he has
a right to think his judgement better than that of any person, or
any multitude, who have not gone through a similar process.

It is not too much to require that what the wisest of mankind, 8
those who are best entitled to trust their own judgement, find
necessary to warrant their relying on it, should be submitted to
by that miscellaneous collection of a few wise and many foolish
individuals, called the public. The most intolerant of churches, the
Roman Catholic Church, even at the canonization of a saint,
admits, and listens patiently to, a "devil's advocate." The holiest
of men, it appears, cannot be admitted to posthumous honours,
until all that the devil could say against him is known and
weighed. If even the Newtonian philosophy were not permitted
to be questioned, mankind could not feel as complete assurance
of its truth as they now do. The beliefs which we have most
warrant for, have no safeguard to rest on, but a standing
invitation to the whole world to prove them unfounded. If the
challenge is not accepted, or is accepted and the attempt fails,
we are far enough from certainty still; but we have done the best
that the existing state of human reason admits of; we have
neglected nothing that could give the truth a chance of reaching

us: if the lists are kept open, we may hope that if there be a better truth, it will be found when the human mind is capable of receiving it; and in the meantime we may rely on having attained such approach to truth, as is possible in our own day. This is the amount of certainty attainable by a fallible being, and this the sole way of attaining it.

Strange it is, that men should admit the validity of the   9
arguments for free discussion, but object to their being "pushed to an extreme"; not seeing that unless the reasons are good for an extreme case, they are not good for any case. Strange that they should imagine that they are not assuming infallibility, when they acknowledge that there should be free discussion on all subjects which can possibly be *doubtful*, but think that some particular principle or doctrine should be forbidden to be questioned because it is so *certain*, that is, because *they are certain* that it is certain. To call any proposition certain, while there is any one who would deny its certainty if permitted, but who is not permitted, is to assume that we ourselves, and those who agree with us, are the judges of certainty, and judges without hearing the other side.

In the present age—which has been described as "destitute of   10
faith, but terrified at scepticism"—in which people feel sure, not so much that their opinions are true, as that they should not know what to do without them—the claims of an opinion to be protected from public attack are rested not so much on its truth, as on its importance to society. There are, it is alleged, certain beliefs, so useful, not to say indispensable to well-being, that it is as much the duty of governments to uphold those beliefs, as to protect any other of the interests of society. In a case of such necessity, and so directly in the line of their duty, something less than infallibility may, it is maintained, warrant, and even bind, governments, to act on their own opinion, confirmed by the general opinion of mankind. It is also often argued, and still oftener thought, that none but bad men would desire to weaken these salutary beliefs; and there can be nothing wrong, it is thought, in restraining bad men, and prohibiting what only such men would wish to practise. This mode of thinking makes the justification of restraints on discussion not a question of the truth of doctrines, but of their usefulness; and flatters itself by that means to escape the responsibility of claiming to be an infallible judge of opinions. But those who thus satisfy themselves, do not perceive that the assumption of infallibility is merely shifted from

one point to another. The usefulness of an opinion is itself matter of opinion: as disputable, as open to discussion, and requiring discussion as much, as the opinion itself. There is the same need of an infallible judge of opinions to decide an opinion to be noxious, as to decide it to be false, unless the opinion condemned has full opportunity of defending itself. And it will not do to say that the heretic may be allowed to maintain the utility or harmlessness of his opinion, though forbidden to maintain its truth. The truth of an opinion is part of its utility. If we would know whether or not it is desirable that a proposition should be believed, is it possible to exclude the consideration of whether or not it is true? In the opinion, not of bad men, but of the best men, no belief which is contrary to truth can be really useful: and can you prevent such men from urging that plea, when they are charged with culpability for denying some doctrine which they are told is useful, but which they believe to be false? Those who are on the side of received opinions, never fail to take all possible advantage of this plea; you do not find *them* handling the question of utility as if it could be completely abstracted from that of truth: on the contrary, it is, above all, because their doctrine is "the truth," that the knowledge or the belief of it is held to be so indispensable. There can be no fair discussion of the question of usefulness, when an argument so vital may be employed on one side, but not on the other. And in point of fact, when law or public feeling do not permit the truth of an opinion to be disputed, they are just as little tolerant of a denial of its usefulness. The utmost they allow is an extenuation of its absolute necessity, or of the positive guilt of rejecting it.

Jessica Mitford

■ ■ ■

The Story of Service

Jessica Mitford (1917–1996), "Queen of the muckrakers," was born in Gloucestershire, England, grew up in an ristocratic British family of seven children, and was educated at home. At nineteen she eloped with her first husband, Esmond Romilly, Winston Churchill's nephew, to fight the Fascists in Spain, before emigrating in 1939 to the United States. Mitford was widowed in 1941 when Romilly was killed in action. Committed to socialist thinking, she became a member of the Communist Party, where she met and then married labour lawyer Robert Treuhaft in 1943. They settled in California. Because of her husband's concern for his clients, whose union benefits went to pay for family funerals, she wrote her most famous book, *The American Way of Death* (1963), which satirically exposes the practices of the American funeral industry. This book launched her reputation as a muckraker and preceded her exposés of the American prison system, in *Kind and Usual Punishment: The Prison Business* (1973) and American obstetrical care, in *The American Way of Birth* (1992). She wrote, "You may not be able to change the world, but at least you can embarrass the guilty." The following is Chapter Two of *The American Way of Death*.

There was a time when the undertaker's tasks were clearcut 1 and rather obvious, and when he billed his patrons accordingly. Typical late 19th century charges, in addition to the price of merchandise, are shown on bills of the period as: 'Services at the house (placing corpse in the coffin), $1.25,' 'Preserving remains on ice, $10,' 'Getting Permit, $1.50.' It was customary for the undertaker to add a few dollars to his bill for being 'in attendance,' which seems only fair and right. The cost of embalming was around $10 in 1880. An undertaker, writing in 1900, recommends these minimums for service charges: Washing and dressing, $5; embalming, $10; hearse, $8 to $10. As historians of the trade have pointed out: 'The undertaker had as yet to conceive of the value of personal services offered professionally for a fee, legitimately claimed.' Well, he has now so conceived with a vengeance.

When weaving in the story of service as it is rendered today, 2
spokesmen for the funeral industry tend to become so carried
away by their own enthusiasm, so positively lyrical and copious
in their declarations, that the outsider may have a little trouble
understanding it all. There are indeed contradictions. Preferred
Funeral Directors International has prepared a mimeographed
talk designed to inform people about service: 'The American
public receive the services of employees and proprietor alike,
nine and one half days of labor for every funeral handled, they
receive the use of automobiles and hearses, a building including
a chapel and other rooms which require building maintenance,
insurance, taxes and licenses, and depreciation, as well as heat
in the winter, cooling in the summer and light and water.' It goes
on to say that while the process of embalming takes only about
three hours, yet, 'it would be necessary for one man to work two
forty-hour weeks to complete a funeral service. This is coupled
with an additional forty hours service required by members of
other local allied professions, including the work of the
cemeteries, newspapers, and of course, the most important of
all, the service of your clergyman. These some 120 hours of labor
are the basic value on which the cost of funerals rests.'

Our informant has lumped a lot of things together here. To 3
start with 'the most important of all, the service of your
clergyman,' the average religious funeral service lasts no more
than 25 minutes. Furthermore, it is not, of course, paid for by the
funeral director. The 'work of the cemeteries' presumably means
the opening and closing of a grave. This now mechanized
operation, which takes 15 to 20 minutes, is likewise not billed as
part of the funeral director's costs. The work of 'newspapers'?
This is a puzzler. Presumably reference is made here to the
publication of an obituary notice on the vital statistics page. It
is, incidentally, surprising to learn that newspaper work is
considered an 'allied profession.'

Just how insurance, taxes, licences and depreciation are 4
figured in as part of the 120 man-hours of service is hard to tell.
The writer does mention that his operation features '65 items of
service.' In general, the funeral salesman is inclined to chuck in
everything he does under the heading of 'service.' For example,
in a typical list of 'services' he will include items like 'securing
statistical data' (in other words, completing the death certificate
and finding out how much insurance was left by the deceased),
'the arrangements conference' (in which the sale of the funeral

to the survivors is made), and the 'keeping of records,' by which he means his own bookkeeping work. Evidently there is some confusion here between items that properly belong in a cost-accounting system and items of *actual* service rendered in any given funeral. In all likelihood, idle time of employees is figured in and prorated as part of the 'man-hours.' The up-to-date funeral home operates on a 24-hour basis, and the mimeographed speech contains the heartening news:

'The funeral service profession of the United States is proud 5 of the fact that there is not a person within the continental limits of the United States who is more than two hours away from a licensed funeral director and embalmer in case of need. That's one that even the fire fighting apparatus of our country cannot match.'

While the hit-or-miss rhetoric of the foregoing is fairly 6 typical of the prose style of the funeral trade as a whole, and while the statement that 120 man-hours are devoted to a single man- (or woman-) funeral may be open to question, there really is a fantastic amount of service accorded the dead body and its survivors.

Having decreed what sort of funeral is right, proper and nice, 7 and having gradually appropriated to himself all the functions connected with it, the funeral director has become responsible for a multitude of tasks beyond the obvious one of 'placing corpse in the coffin' recorded in our 19th century funeral bill. His self-imposed duties fall into two main categories: attention to the corpse itself, and the stage-managing of the funeral.

The drama begins to unfold with the arrival of the corpse at 8 the mortuary.

Alas, poor Yorick! How *very* surprised he would be to see 9 how his counterpart of today is whisked off to a funeral parlour and is in short order sprayed, sliced, pierced, pickled, trussed, trimmed, creamed, waxed, painted, rouged and neatly dressed—transformed from a common corpse into a Beautiful Memory Picture. This process is known in the trade as embalming and restorative art, and is so universally employed in the United States and Canada that the funeral director does it routinely, without consulting corpse or kin. He regards as eccentric those few who are hardy enough to suggest that it might be dispensed with. Yet no law requires embalming, no religious doctrine commends it, nor is it dictated by considerations of health, sanitation, or even of personal daintiness. In no part of the world

but in Northern America is it widely used. The purpose of
embalming is to make the corpse presentable for viewing in a
suitably costly container; and here too the funeral director
routinely, without first consulting the family, prepares the body
for public display.

Is all this legal? The processes to which a dead body may be   10
subjected are after all to some extent circumscribed by law. In
most states, for instance, the signature of next of kin must be
obtained before an autopsy may be performed, before the
deceased may be cremated, before the body may be turned over
to a medical school for research purposes; or such provision must
be made in the decedent's will. In the case of embalming, no such
permission is required nor is it ever sought. A textbook, *Principles
and Practices of Embalming*, comments on this: 'There is some
question regarding the legality of much that is done within the
preparation room.' The author points out that it would be most
unusual for a responsible member of a bereaved family to instruct
the mortician, in so many words, to *'embalm'* the body of a
deceased relative. The very term 'embalming' is so seldom used
that the mortician must rely upon custom in the matter. The
author concludes that unless the family specifies otherwise, the
act of entrusting the body to the care of a funeral establishment
carries with it an implied permission to go ahead and embalm.

Embalming is indeed a most extraordinary procedure, and   11
one must wonder at the docility of Americans who each year
pay hundreds of millions of dollars for its perpetuation, blissfully
ignorant of what it is all about, what is done, how it is done. Not
one in ten thousand has any idea of what actually takes place.
Books on the subject are extremely hard to come by. They are
not to be found in libraries or bookshops.

In an era when huge television audiences watch surgical   12
operations in the comfort of their living rooms, when, thanks to
the animated cartoon, the geography of the digestive system has
become familiar territory even to the nursery-school set, in a land
where the satisfaction of curiosity about almost all matters is a
national pastime, the secrecy surrounding embalming can, surely,
hardly be attributed to the inherent gruesomeness of the subject.
Custom in this regard has within this century suffered a complete
reversal. In the early days of American embalming, when it was
performed in the home of the deceased, it was almost mandatory
for some relative to stay by the embalmer's side and witness the
procedure. Today, family members who might wish to be in

attendance would certainly be dissuaded by the funeral director. All others, except apprentices, are excluded by law from the preparation room.

A close look at what does actually take place may explain in 13 large measure the undertaker's intractable reticence concerning a procedure that has become his major *raison d'être*. Is it possible he fears that public information about embalming might lead patrons to wonder if this trip is really necessary? If the funeral men are loath to discuss the subject outside the trade, the reader may, understandably, be equally loath to go on reading at this point. For those who have the stomach for it, let us part the formaldehyde curtain and find out what happens. Others should skip to [paragraph 24].

The body is first laid out in the undertaker's morgue—or 14 rather, as the trade prefers, Mr. Jones is reposing in the preparation room—to be readied to bid the world farewell.

The preparation room in any of the better funeral 15 establishments has the tiled and sterile look of a surgery, and indeed the embalmer-restorative artist who does his chores there is beginning to adopt the term 'dermasurgeon' (appropriately corrupted by some mortician-writers as 'demi-surgeon') to describe his calling. His equipment, consisting of scalpels, scissors, augers, forceps, clamps, needles, pumps, tubes, bowls and basins, is crudely imitative of the surgeon's, as is his technique, acquired in a nine- or twelve-month post-high-school course in an embalming school. He is supplied by an advanced chemical industry with a bewildering array of fluids, sprays, pastes, oils, powders, creams, to fix or soften tissue, shrink or distend it as needed, dry it here, restore the moisture there. There are cosmetics, waxes and paints to fill and cover features, even plaster of Paris to replace entire limbs. There are ingenious aids to prop and stabilize the cadaver: a Vari-Pose Head Rest, the Edwards Arm and Hand Positioner, the Repose Block (to support the shoulders during the embalming), and the Throop foot positioner, which resembles an old-fashioned stocks.

Mr. John H. Eckels, president of the Eckels College of Mortuary 16 Science, thus describes the first part of the embalming procedure: 'In the hands of a skilled practitioner, this work may be done in a comparatively short time and without mutilating the body other than by slight incision—so slight that it scarcely would cause serious inconvenience if made upon a living person. It is necessary to remove the blood, and doing this not only helps in the disinfecting, but removes the principal cause of disfigurements due to discoloration.' This is a plucky try at reassurance, although some living persons might think it *would* cause a rather serious inconvenience to remove their blood.

Another textbook discusses the all-important time element: 17
'The earlier this is done, the better, for every hour that elapses between death and embalming will add to the problems and complications encountered. . . .' Just how soon should one get going on the embalming? The author tells us: 'On the basis of such scanty information made available to this profession through its rudimentary and haphazard system of technical research, we must conclude that the best results are to be obtained if the subject is embalmed before life is completely extinct—-that is, before cellular death has occurred. In the average case, this would mean within an hour after somatic death.' For those who feel that there is something a little rudimentary, not to say haphazard, about this advice, a comforting thought is offered by another writer. Speaking of fears entertained in early days of premature burial, he points out: 'One of the effects of embalming by chemical injection, however, has been to dispel fears of live burial.' How true; once the blood is removed, chances of live burial are indeed remote.

To return to Mr. Jones, the blood is drained out through the   18
veins and replaced by embalming fluid pumped in through the arteries. As noted in *Principles and Practices of Embalming*, 'every operator has a favorite injection and drainage point—a fact which becomes a handicap only if he fails or refuses to forsake his favorites when conditions demand it.' Typical favourites are the carotid artery, femoral artery, jugular vein, subclavian vein. There are various choices of embalming fluid. If Flextone is used, it will produce a 'mild, flexible rigidity. The skin retains a velvety softness, the tissues are rubbery and pliable. Ideal for women and children.' It may be blended with B. and G. Products Company's Lyf-Lyk tint, which is guaranteed to reproduce 'nature's own skin texture . . . the velvety appearance of living tissue.' Suntone comes in three separate tints: Suntan; Special Cosmetic Tint, a pink shade 'especially indicated for young female subjects'; and Regular Cosmetic Tint, moderately pink.

About three to six gallons of a dyed and perfumed solution   19
of formaldehyde, glycerin, borax, phenol, alcohol and water are soon circulating through Mr. Jones, whose mouth has been sewn together with a 'needle directed upward between the upper lip and gum and brought out through the left nostril,' with the

corners raised slightly 'for a more pleasant expression.' If he should be bucktoothed, his teeth are cleaned with Bon Ami and coated with colourless nail polish. His eyes, meanwhile, are closed with flesh-tinted eye caps and eye cement.

The next step is to have at Mr. Jones with a trocar, a long, 20 hollow needle attached to a tube. It is jabbed into the abdomen, poked around the entrails and chest cavity, the contents of which are pumped out and replaced with 'cavity fluid.' This done, and the hole in the abdomen sewn up, Mr. Jones's face is heavily creamed (to protect the skin from burns which may be caused by leakage of the chemicals), and he is covered with a sheet and left unmolested for a while. But not for long—there is more, much more, in store for him. He has been embalmed, but not yet restored, and the best time to start the restorative work is eight to ten hours after embalming, when the tissues have become firm and dry.

The object of all this attention to the corpse, it must be 21 remembered, is to make it presentable for viewing in an attitude of healthy repose. 'Our customs require the presentation of our dead in the semblance of normality . . . unmarred by the ravages of illness, disease or mutilation,' says Mr. J. Sheridan Mayer in his *Restorative Art*. This is rather a large order since few people die in the full bloom of health, unravaged by illness and unmarked by some disfigurement. The funeral industry is equal to the challenge: 'In some cases the gruesome appearance of a mutilated or disease-ridden subject may be quite discouraging. The task of restoration may seem impossible and shake the confidence of the embalmer. This is the time for intestinal fortitude and determination. Once the formative work is begun and affected tissues are cleaned or removed, all doubts of success vanish. It is surprising and gratifying to discover the results which may be obtained.'

The embalmer, having allowed an appropriate interval to 22 elapse, returns to the attack, but now he brings into play the skill and equipment of sculptor and cosmetician. Is a hand missing? Casting one in plaster of Paris is a simple matter. 'For replacement purposes, only a cast of the back of the hand is necessary; this is within the ability of the average operator and is quite adequate.' If a lip or two, a nose or an ear should be missing, the embalmer has at hand a variety of restorative waxes with which to model replacements. Pores and skin texture are simulated by stippling with a little brush, and over this cosmetics are laid on. Head off?

Decapitation cases are rather routinely handled. Ragged edges are trimmed, and head joined to torso with a series of splints, wires and sutures. It is a good idea to have a little something at the neck—a scarf or high collar—when time for viewing comes. Swollen mouth? Cut out tissue as needed from inside the lips. If too much is removed, the surface contour can easily be restored by padding with cotton. Swollen necks and cheeks are reduced by removing tissue through vertical incisions made down each side of the neck. 'When the deceased is casketed, the pillow will hide the suture incisions . . . as an extra precaution against leakage, the suture may be painted with liquid sealer.'

The opposite condition is more likely to present itself—that of emaciation. His hypodermic syringe now loaded with massage cream, the embalmer seeks out and fills the hollowed and sunken areas by injection. In this procedure the backs of the hands and fingers and the under-chin area should not be neglected. 23

Positioning the lips is a problem that recurrently challenges the ingenuity of the embalmer. Closed too tightly, they tend to give a stern, even disapproving, expression. Ideally, embalmers feel, the lips should give the impression of being ever so slightly parted, the upper lip protruding slightly for a more youthful appearance. This takes some engineering, however, as the lips tend to drift apart. Lip drift can sometimes be remedied by pushing one or two straight pins through the inner margin of the lower lip and then inserting them between the two front upper teeth. If Mr. Jones happens to have no teeth, the pins can just as easily be anchored in his Armstrong Face Former and Denture Replacer. Another method to maintain lip closure is to dislocate the lower jaw, which is then held in its new position by a wire run through holes which have been drilled through the upper and lower jaws at the midline. As the French are fond of saying, *il faut souffrir pour être belle.*[1] 24

If Mr. Jones has died of jaundice, the embalming fluid will very likely turn him green. Does this deter the embalmer? Not if he has intestinal fortitude. Masking pastes and cosmetics are heavily laid on, burial garments and casket interiors are colour-correlated with particular care, and Jones is displayed beneath rose-coloured lights. Friends will say, 'How *well* he looks.' Death 25

---

[1][Mitford's note] In 1963, *Mortuary Management* reports a new development: 'Natural Expression Formers,' an invention of Funeral Directors Research Company. 'They may be used to replace one or both artificial dentures, or over natural teeth; have "bite-indicator" lines as a closure guide . . . Natural Expression Formers also offer more control of facial expression.'

by carbon monoxide, on the other hand, can be rather a good thing from the embalmer's viewpoint: 'One advantage is the fact that this type of discoloration is an exaggerated form of a natural pink coloration.' This is nice because the healthy glow is already present and needs but little attention.

The patching and filling completed, Mr. Jones is now shaved, washed and dressed. Cream-based cosmetic, available in pink, flesh, suntan, brunette and blond, is applied to his hands and face, his hair is shampooed and combed (and, in the case of Mrs. Jones, set), his hands manicured. For the horny-handed son of toil special care must be taken; cream should be applied to remove ingrained grime, and the nails cleaned. 'If he were not in the habit of having them manicured in life, trimming and shaping is advised for better appearance—never questioned by kin.'   26

Jones is now ready for casketing (this is the present participle of the verb 'to casket'). In this operation his right shoulder should be depressed slightly 'to turn the body a bit to the right and soften the appearance of lying flat on the back.' Positioning the hands is a matter of importance, and special rubber positioning blocks may be used. The hands should be cupped slightly for a more lifelike, relaxed appearance. Proper placement of the body requires a delicate sense of balance. It should lie as high as possible in the casket, yet not so high that the lid, when lowered, will hit the nose. On the other hand, we are cautioned, placing the body too low 'creates the impression that the body is in a box.'   27

Jones is next wheeled into the appointed slumber room where a few last touches may be added—his favourite pipe placed in his hand or, if he was a great reader, a book propped into position. (In the case of little Master Jones a Teddy bear may be clutched.) Here he will hold open house for a few days, visiting hours 10 a.m. to 9 p.m.   28

All now being in readiness, the funeral director is discreetly scurrying around to see that all goes as it should. A staff conference is called to make sure that each assistant knows his precise duties. Mr. Wilber Krieger writes: 'This makes your staff feel that they are a part of the team, with a definite assignment that must be properly carried out if the whole plan is to succeed. You never heard of a football coach who failed to talk to his entire team before they go on the field. They have drilled on the plays they are to execute for hours and days, and yet the successful coach knows the importance of making even the bench-warming third-string substitute feel that   29

he is important if the game is to be won.' The winning of *this* game
is predicated upon glass-smooth handling of the logistics. The
funeral director has notified the pallbearers whose names were
furnished by the family, has arranged for the presence of clergyman,
organist, and soloist, has provided transportation for everybody, has
organized and listed the flowers sent by friends. In *Psychology of
Funeral Service* Mr. Edward A. Martin points out: 'He may not
always do as much as the family thinks he is doing, but it is his
helpful guidance that they appreciate in knowing they are
proceeding as they should. . . . The important thing is how well his
services can be used to make the family believe they are giving
unlimited expression to their own sentiment.'

The religious service may be held in a church or in the chapel   30
in the funeral home; the funeral director vastly prefers the latter
arrangement, for not only is it more convenient for him but it
affords him the opportunity to show off his beautiful facilities
to the gathered mourners. After the clergyman has had his say,
the mourners queue up to file past the casket for a last look at
the deceased. The family is *never* asked whether they want an
open-casket ceremony; in the absence of their instruction to the
contrary, this is taken for granted. Consequently well over 90
per cent of all American funerals feature the open casket—a
custom unknown in other parts of the world. Foreigners are
astonished by it. An Englishwoman living in San Francisco
described her reaction in a letter to the writer:

> I myself have attended only one funeral here—that of an elderly
> fellow worker of mine. After the service I could not understand
> why everyone was walking towards the coffin (sorry, I mean
> casket), but thought I had better follow the crowd. It shook me
> rigid to get there and find the casket open and poor old Oscar
> lying there in his brown tweed suit, wearing a suntan makeup
> and just the wrong shade of lipstick. If I had not been extremely
> fond of the old boy, I have a horrible feeling that I might have
> giggled. Then and there I decided that I could never face
> another American funeral—even dead.

The casket (which has been resting throughout the service   31
on a Classic Beauty Ultra Metal Casket Bier) is now transported
by a hydraulically operated device called Porto-Lift to a
balloon-tyred, Glide Easy casket carriage which will wheel it to
yet another conveyance, the Cadillac Funeral Coach. This may
be lavender, cream, light green—anything but black. Interiors,

of course, are colour-correlated, 'for the man who cannot stop short of perfection.'

At graveside, the casket is lowered into the earth. This office, 32 once the prerogative of friends of the deceased, is now performed by a patented mechanical lowering device. A 'Lifetime Green' artificial grass mat is at the ready to conceal the sere earth, and overhead, to conceal the sky, is a portable Steril Chapel Tent ('resists the intense heat and humidity of summer and the terrific storms of winter . . . available in Silver Grey, Rose or Evergreen'). Now is the time for the ritual scattering of earth over the coffin, as the solemn words 'earth to earth, ashes to ashes, dust to dust' are pronounced by the officiating cleric. This can today be accomplished 'with a mere flick of the wrist with the Gordon Leak-Proof Earth Dispenser. No grasping of a handful of dirt, no soiled fingers. Simple, dignified, beautiful, reverent! The modern way!' The Gordon Earth Dispenser (at $5) is of nickel-plated brass construction. It is not only 'attractive to the eye and long wearing'; it is also 'one of the "tools" for building better public relations' if presented as 'an appropriate non-commercial gift' to the clergyman. It is shaped something like a saltshaker.

Untouched by human hand, the casket and the earth are 33 now united.

It is in the function of directing the participants through this 34 maze of gadgetry that the funeral director has assigned to himself his relatively new role of 'grief therapist.' He has relieved the family of every detail, he has revamped the corpse to look like a living doll, he has arranged for it to nap for a few days in a slumber room, he has put on a well-oiled performance in which the concept of *death* has played no part whatsoever—unless it was inconsiderately mentioned by the clergyman who conducted the religious service. He has done everything in his power to make the funeral a real pleasure for everybody concerned. He and his team have given their all to score an upset victory over death.

Dale Carnegie has decreed that in the lexicon of the successful 35 man there is no such word as 'failure.' So have the funeral men managed to delete the word 'death' and all its associations from their vocabulary. They have from time to time published lists of In and Out words and phrases to be memorized and used in connection with the final return of dust to dust; then, still dissatisfied with the result, have elaborated and revised the lists. Thus a 1916 glossary substitutes 'prepare body' for 'handle corpse.' Today, though, 'body' is Out and 'remains' or 'Mr. Jones' is In.

'The use of improper terminology by anyone affiliated with   36
a mortuary should be strictly forbidden,' declares Edward A.
Martin. He suggests a rather thorough overhauling of the
language; his deathless words include: 'service, not funeral; Mr.,
Mrs., Miss Blank, not corpse or body; preparation room, not
morgue; casket, not coffin; funeral director or mortician, not
undertaker; reposing room or slumber room, not laying-out room;
display room, not showroom; baby or infant, not still-born;
deceased, not dead; autopsy or post-mortem, not post; casket
coach, not hearse; shipping case, not shipping box; flower car,
not flower truck; cremains or cremated remains, not ashes;
clothing, dress, suit etc., not shroud; drawing room, not parlor.'

This rather basic list was refined in 1956 by Victor Landig in   37
his *Basic Principles of Funeral Service.* He enjoins the reader to
avoid using the word 'death' as much as possible, even sometimes
when such avoidance may seem impossible; for example, a death
certificate should be referred to as a 'vital statistics form.' One
should speak not of the 'job' but rather of the 'call.' We do not
'haul' a dead person, we 'transfer' or 'remove' him—and we do
this in a 'service car,' not a 'body car.' We 'open and close' his
grave rather than dig and fill it, and in it we 'inter' rather than
bury him. This is done not in a graveyard or cemetery but rather
in a 'memorial park.' The deceased is beautified, not with
makeup, but with 'cosmetics.' Anyway, he didn't die, he 'expired.'
An important error to guard against, cautions Mr. Landig, is
referring to 'cost of the casket.' The phrase 'amount of investment
in the service' is a wiser usage here.

Miss Anne Hamilton Franz, writing in *Funeral Direction and*   38
Management, adds an interesting footnote on the use of the word
'ashes' to describe (in a word) ashes. She fears this usage will
encourage scattering (for what is more natural than to scatter
ashes?) and prefers to speak of 'cremated remains' or 'human
remains.' She does not like the word 'retort' to describe the
container in which cremation takes place, but prefers 'cremation
chamber' or 'cremation vault,' because this 'sounds better and
softens any harshness to sensitive feelings.'

As for the Loved One, poor fellow, he wanders like a sad   39
ghost through the funeral men's pronouncements. No provision
seems to have been made for the burial of a Heartily Disliked
One, although the necessity for such must arise in the course of
human events.

George Orwell

■■■

Politics and the English Language

George Orwell (1903–1950), journalist, essayist, novelist, was born Eric
Arthur Blair in Motihari, Bengal, India, of English parents. Blair grew up
and attended school in England, leaving in 1921 the prestigious Eton
College which he had attended on scholarship and in 1922 returning to
Asia as a member of the Indian Imperial Police in Burma. After five years,
increasingly cynical about the role of the British in India, Blair quit to become a writer. He adopted the name George Orwell for the publication
of his first book, *Down and Out in Paris and London* (1933), which was based
on the eight difficult years that followed his sojourn in Burma, which was
the subject of his next book, *Burmese Days* (1934); several of his subsequent
works, including *The Road to Wigan Pier* (1937) and *Homage to Catalonia*
(1938), are also based on firsthand experience. Orwell's literary career includes several more novels and hundreds of essays and articles, but he is
probably best known for the two political satires that attack totalitarianism,
Animal Farm (1945) and *Nineteen Eighty-Four* (1950). Both works give brilliant expression to many of the ideas that govern his essays, expressing
his dictum as a writer to fight social injustice, oppression, political tyranny,
and totalitarianism in any form. Many of his essays are notable for the ar-
ticulation of these ideals, both literary and political, among them "Shooting
an Elephant," "A Hanging," "How the Poor Die," and "Why I Write"; but
probably his most oft-reprinted essay is the one which follows. Written
in 1946, "Politics and the English Language" prefigures *Nineteen Eighty-
Four* in several interesting ways, in that it links the power of words with the
power of governments, and illustrates the dangers of language that ob-
fuscates meaning, intentionally or not. Itself an example of the clear, plain
writing it argues for, this classic piece of twentieth-century writing was
first published in *The New Republic* in June 1946.

■⸻⸻⸻⸻⸻⸻⸻⸻⸻⸻⸻⸻■

Most people who bother with the matter at all would admit   1
that the English language is in a bad way, but it is generally
assumed that we cannot by conscious action do anything about
it. Our civilization is decadent and our language—so the argument runs—must inevitably share in the general collapse. It follows that any struggle against the abuse of language is a

sentimental archaism, like preferring candles to electric light or hansom cabs to aeroplanes. Underneath this lies the half-conscious belief that language is a natural growth and not an instrument which we shape for our own purposes.

Now, it is clear that the decline of a language must ultimately 2 have political and economic causes: it is not due simply to the bad influence of this or that individual writer. But an effect can become a cause, reinforcing the original cause and producing the same effect in an intensified form, and so on indefinitely. A man may take to drink because he feels himself to be a failure, and then fail all the more completely because he drinks. It is rather the same thing that is happening to the English language. It becomes ugly and inaccurate because our thoughts are foolish, but the slovenliness of our language makes it easier for us to have foolish thoughts. The point is that the process is reversible. Modern English, especially written English, is full of bad habits which spread by imitation and which can be avoided if one is willing to take the necessary trouble. If one gets rid of these habits one can think more clearly, and to think clearly is a necessary first step toward political regeneration: so that the fight against bad English is not frivolous and is not the exclusive concern of professional writers. I will come back to this presently, and I hope that by that time the meaning of what I have said here will have become clearer. Meanwhile, here are five specimens of the English language as it is now habitually written.

These five passages have not been picked out because they are 3 especially bad—I could have quoted far worse if I had chosen— but because they illustrate various of the mental vices from which we now suffer. They are a little below the average, but are fairly representative samples. I number them so that I can refer back to them when necessary:

> (1) I am not, indeed, sure whether it is not true to say that the Milton who once seemed not unlike a seventeenth-century Shelley had not become, out of an experience ever more bitter in each year, more alien [*sic*] to the founder of that Jesuit sect which nothing could induce him to tolerate.
>
> Professor Harold Laski
(Essay in *Freedom of Expression*).

> (2) Above all, we cannot play ducks and drakes with a native battery of idioms which prescribes such egregious collocations

of vocables as the Basic *put up with* for *tolerate*, or *put at a loss* for *bewilder*.

Professor Lancelot Hogben (*Interglossa*).

(3) On the one side we have the free personality: by definition it is not neurotic, for it has neither conflict nor dream. Its desires, such as they are, are transparent, for they are just what institutional approval keeps in the forefront of consciousness; another institutional pattern would alter their number and intensity; there is little in them that is natural, irreducible, or culturally dangerous. But *on the other side*, the social bond itself is nothing but the mutual reflection of these self-secure integrities. Recall the definition of love. Is not this the very picture of a small academic? Where is there a place in this hall of mirrors for either personality or fraternity?

Essay on psychology in *Politics* (New York).

(4) All the "best people" from the gentlemen's clubs, and all the frantic fascist captains, united in common hatred of Socialism and bestial horror at the rising tide of the mass revolutionary movement, have turned to acts of provocation, to foul incendiarism, to medieval legends of poisoned wells, to legalize their own destruction of proletarian organizations, and rouse the agitated petty-bourgeoise to chauvinistic fervor on behalf of the fight against the revolutionary way out of the crisis.

Communist pamphlet.

(5) If a new spirit *is* to be infused into this old country, there is one thorny and contentious reform which must be tackled, and that is the humanization and galvanization of the B.B.C. Timidity here will bespeak canker and atrophy of the soul. The heart of Britain may be sound and of strong beat, for instance, but the British lion's roar at present is like that of Bottom in Shakespeare's *Midsummer Night's Dream*—as gentle as any sucking dove. A virile new Britain cannot continue indefinitely to be traduced in the eyes or rather ears, of the world by the effete languors of Langham Place, brazenly masquerading as "standard English." When the Voice of Britain is heard at nine o'clock, better far and infinitely less ludicrous to hear aitches honestly dropped than the present priggish, inflated, inhibited, school-ma'amish arch braying of blameless bashful mewing maidens!

Letter in *Tribune.*

Each of these passages has faults of its own, but, quite apart   4
from avoidable ugliness, two qualities are common to all of them.
The first is staleness of imagery; the other is lack of precision.
The writer either has a meaning and cannot express it, or he
inadvertently says something else, or he is almost indifferent as
to whether his words mean anything or not. This mixture of
vagueness and sheer incompetence is the most marked
characteristic of modern English prose, and especially of any
kind of political writing. As soon as certain topics are raised, the
concrete melts into the abstract and no one seems able to think of
turns of speech that are not hackneyed: prose consists less and less
of *words* chosen for the sake of their meaning, and more and more
of *phrases* tacked together like the sections of a prefabricated
henhouse. I list below, with notes and examples, various of the
tricks by means of which the work of prose-construction is
habitually dodged:

Dying metaphors. A newly invented metaphor assists thought   5
by evoking a visual image, while on the other hand a metaphor
which is technically "dead" (e.g. *iron resolution*) has in effect
reverted to being an ordinary word and can generally be used
without loss of vividness. But in between these two classes there
is a huge dump of worn-out metaphors which have lost all
evocative power and are merely used because they save people
the trouble of inventing phrases for themselves. Examples are:
*Ring the changes on, take up the cudgels for, toe the line, ride
roughshod over, stand shoulder to shoulder with, play into the hands
of, no axe to grind, grist to the mill, fishing in troubled waters, on
the order of the day, Achilles' heel, swan song, hotbed.* Many of these
are used without knowledge of their meaning (what is a "rift,"
for instance?), and incompatible metaphors are frequently
mixed, a sure sign that the writer is not interested in what he is
saying. Some metaphors now current have been twisted out of
their original meaning without those who use them even being
aware of the fact. For example, *toe the line* is sometimes written
as *tow the line.* Another example is *the hammer and the anvil,* now
always used with the implication that the anvil gets the worst of
it. In real life it is always the anvil that breaks the hammer,
never the other way about: a writer who stopped to think what
he was saying would be aware of this, and would avoid
perverting the original phrase.

Operators or *verbal false limbs.* These save the trouble of picking 6
out appropriate verbs and nouns, and at the same time pad each
sentence with extra syllables which give it an appearance of
symmetry. Characteristic phrases are *render inoperative, militate
against, make contact with, be subjected to, give rise to, give grounds for,
have the effect of, play a leading part (role) in, make itself felt, take effect,
exhibit a tendency to, serve the purpose of, etc., etc.* The keynote is the
elimination of simple verbs. Instead of being a single word, such
as *break, stop, spoil, mend, kill,* a verb becomes a *phrase,* made up of
a noun or adjective tacked on to some general-purposes verb such
as *prove, serve, form, play, render.* In addition, the passive voice is
wherever possible used in preference to the active, and noun
constructions are used instead of gerunds (*by examination of* instead
of *by examining*). The range of verbs is further cut down by means
of the *-ize* and *de-* formations, and the banal statements are given
an appearance of profundity by means of the *not un-* formation.
Simple conjunctions and prepositions are replaced by such phrases
as *with respect to, having regard to, the fact that, by dint of, in view of,
in the interests of, on the hypothesis that*; and the ends of sentences are
saved from anticlimax by such resounding commonplaces as
*greatly to be desired, cannot be left out of account, a development to be
expected in the near future, deserving of serious consideration, brought
to a satisfactory conclusion,* and so on and so forth.

Pretentious diction. Words like *phenomenon, element, individual* 7
(as noun), *objective, categorical, effective, virtual, basic, primary,
promote, constitute, exhibit, exploit, utilize, eliminate, liquidate,* are
used to dress up a simple statement and give an air of scientific
impartiality to biased judgements. Adjectives like *epoch-making,
epic, historic, unforgettable, triumphant, age-old, inevitable, inexorable,
veritable,* are used to dignify the sordid process of international
politics, while writing that aims at glorifying war usually takes on
an archaic color, its characteristic words being: *realm, throne,
chariot, mailed fist, trident, sword, shield, buckler, banner, jackboot,
clarion.* Foreign words and expressions such as *cul de sac, ancien
régime, deus ex machina, mutatis mutandis, status quo, gleichschaltung,
weltanschauung* are used to give an air of culture and elegance.
Except for the useful abbreviations *i.e., e.g.,* and *etc.,* there is no real
need for any of the hundreds of foreign phrases now current in
the English language. Bad writers, and especially scientific,
political, and sociological writers, are nearly always haunted by

the notion that Latin or Greek words are grander than Saxon ones, and unnecessary words like *expedite, ameliorate, predict, extraneous, deracinated, clandestine, subaqueous*, and hundreds of others constantly gain ground from their Anglo-Saxon numbers.[1] The jargon peculiar to Marxist writing (*hyena, hangman, cannibal, petty bourgeois, these gentry, lacquey, flunkey, mad dog, White Guard*, etc.) consists largely of words translated from Russian, German, or French; but the normal way of coining a new word is to use a Latin or Greek root with the appropriate affix and, where necessary, the *–ize* formation. It is often easier to make up words of this kind (*deregionalize, impermissible, extramarital, non-fragmentary* and so forth) than to think up the English words that will cover one's meaning. The result, in general, is an increase in slovenliness and vagueness.

Meaningless words. In certain kinds of writing, particularly   8 in art criticism and literary criticism, it is normal to come across long passages which are almost completely lacking in meaning.[2] Words like *romantic, plastic, values, human, dead, sentimental, natural, vitality*, as used in art criticism, are strictly meaningless, in the sense that they not only do not point to any discoverable object, but are hardly ever expected to do so by the reader. When one critic writes, "The outstanding feature of Mr. X's work is its living quality," while another writes, "The immediately striking thing about Mr. X's work is its peculiar deadness," the reader accepts this as a simple difference of opinion. If words like *black* and *white* were involved, instead of the jargon words *dead* and *living*, he would see at once that language was being used in an improper way. Many political words are similarly abused. The word *Fascism* has now no meaning except in so far as it signifies "something not desirable." The words *democracy, socialism, freedom, patriotic, realistic, justice*, have each of them several different meanings which cannot be reconciled with one another. In the case of a

---

[1] [Orwell's note] An interesting illustration of this is the way in which the English flower names which were in use till very recently are being ousted by Greek ones, *snapdragon* becoming *antirrhinum, forget-me-not* becoming *myosotis*, etc. It is hard to see any practical reason for this change of fashion: it is probably due to an instinctive turning-away from the more homely word and a vague feeling that the Greek word is scientific.

[2] [Orwell's note] Example: "Comfort's catholicity of perception and image, strangely Whitmanesque in range, almost the exact opposite in aesthetic compulsion, continues to evoke that trembling atmospheric accumulative hinting at a cruel, an inexorably serene timelessness. . . . Wrey Gardiner scores by aiming at simple bull's-eyes with precision. Only they are not so simple, and through this contented sadness runs more than the surface bitter-sweet of resignation." (*Poetry Quarterly*.)

word like *democracy,* not only is there no agreed definition, but the attempt to make one is resisted from all sides. It is almost universally felt that when we call a country democratic we are praising it: consequently the defenders of every kind of régime claim that it is a democracy, and fear that they might have to stop using that word if it were tied down to any one meaning. Words of this kind are often used in a consciously dishonest way. That is, the person who uses them has his own private definition, but allows his hearer to think he means something quite different. Statements like *Marshal Pétain was a true patriot, The Soviet press is the freest in the world, The Catholic Church is opposed to persecution,* are almost always made with intent to deceive. Other words used in variable meanings, in most cases more or less dishonestly, are: *class, totalitarian, science, progressive, reactionary, bourgeois, equality.*

Now that I have made this catalogue of swindles and perver- 9
sions, let me give another example of the kind of writing that they lead to. This time it must of its nature be an imaginary one. I am going to translate a passage of good English into modern English of the worst sort. Here is a well-known verse from *Ecclesiastes:*
"I returned and saw under the sun, that the race is not to the 10
swift, nor the battle to the strong, neither yet bread to the wise, nor yet riches to men of understanding, nor yet favour to men of skill; but time and chance happeneth to them all."
Here it is in modern English: 11
"Objective considerations of contemporary phenomena 12
compel the conclusion that success or failure in competitive activities exhibits no tendency to be commensurate with innate capacity, but that a considerable element of the unpredictable must invariably be taken into account."
This is a parody, but not a very gross one. Exhibit (3), above, 13
for instance, contains several patches of the same kind of English. It will be seen that I have not made a full translation. The beginning and ending of the sentence follow the original meaning fairly closely, but in the middle the concrete illustrations—race, battle, bread—dissolve into the vague phrases "success or failure in competitive activities." This had to be so, because no modern writer of the kind I am discussing—no one capable of using phrases like "objective considerations of contemporary phenomena"—would ever tabulate his thoughts in that precise and detailed way. The whole tendency of modern prose is away from concreteness. Now analyse these two sentences a little more

closely. The first contains forty-nine words but only sixty syllables, and all its words are those of everyday life. The second contains thirty-eight words of ninety syllables: eighteen of its words are from Latin roots, and one from Greek. The first sentence contains six vivid images, and only one phrase ("time and chance") that could be called vague. The second contains not a single fresh, arresting phrase, and in spite of its ninety syllables it gives only a shortened version of the meaning contained in the first. Yet without a doubt it is the second kind of sentence that is gaining ground in modern English. I do not want to exaggerate. This kind of writing is not yet universal, and outcrops of simplicity will occur here and there in the worst-written page. Still, if you or I were told to write a few lines on the uncertainty of human fortunes, we should probably come much nearer to my imaginary sentence than to the one from *Ecclesiastes.*

As I have tried to show, modern writing at its worst does 14 not consist in picking out words for the sake of their meaning and inventing images in order to make the meaning clearer. It consists in gumming together long strips of words which have already been set in order by someone else, and making the results presentable by sheer humbug. The attraction of this way of writing is that it is easy. It is easier—even quicker, once you have the habit—to say *In my opinion it is not an unjustifiable assumption that* than to say *I think*. If you use ready-made phrases, you not only don't have to hunt about for the words; you also don't have to bother with the rhythms of your sentences, since these phrases are generally so arranged as to be more or less euphonious. When you are composing in a hurry—when you are dictating to a stenographer, for instance, or making a public speech—it is natural to fall into a pretentious, Latinized style. Tags like *a consideration which we should do well to bear in mind* or *a conclusion to which all of us would readily assent* will save many a sentence from coming down with a bump. By using stale metaphors, similes, and idioms, you save much mental effort, at the cost of leaving your meaning vague, not only for your reader but for yourself. This is the significance of mixed metaphors. The sole aim of a metaphor is to call up a visual image. When these images clash—as in *The Fascist octopus has sung its swan song, the jackboot is thrown into the melting pot*—it can be taken as certain that the writer is not seeing a mental image of the objects he is naming; in other words he is not really thinking. Look again at the examples I gave at the beginning of this essay. Professor Laski (1) uses five negatives in fifty-three words. One of these is superfluous, making nonsense of the whole passage, and in addition there is the slip—*alien* for akin—making further nonsense, and several avoidable pieces of clumsiness which increase the general vagueness. Professor Hogben (2) plays ducks and drakes with a battery which is able to write prescriptions, and, while disapproving of the everyday phrase *put up with,* is unwilling to look *egregious* up in the dictionary and see what it means; (3), if one takes an uncharitable attitude towards it, is simply meaningless: probably one could work out its intended meaning by reading the whole of the article in which it occurs. In (4), the writer knows more or less what he wants to say, but an accumulation of stale phrases chokes him like tea leaves blocking a sink. In (5), words and meaning have almost parted company. People who write in this manner usually have a general emotional meaning—they dislike one thing and want to express solidarity with another—but they are not interested in the detail of what they are saying. A scrupulous writer, in every sentence that he writes, will ask himself at least four questions, thus: What am I trying to say? What words will express it? What image or idiom will make it clearer? Is this image fresh enough to have an effect? And he will probably ask himself two more: Could I put it more shortly? Have I said anything that is avoidably ugly? But you are not obliged to go to all this trouble. You can shirk it by simply throwing your mind open and letting the ready-made phrases come crowding in. They will construct your sentences for you—even think your thoughts for you, to a certain extent—and at need they will perform the important service of partially concealing your meaning even from yourself. It is at this point that the special connection between politics and the debasement of language becomes clear.

In our time it is broadly true that political writing is bad   15 writing. Where it is not true, it will generally be found that the writer is some kind of rebel, expressing his private opinions and not a "party line." Orthodoxy, of whatever color, seems to demand a lifeless, imitative style. The political dialects to be found in pamphlets, leading articles, manifestos, White Papers and the speeches of under-secretaries do, of course, vary from party to party, but they are all alike in that one almost never finds in them a fresh, vivid, home-made turn of speech. When one watches some tired hack on the platform mechanically repeating the familiar phrases—*bestial atrocities, iron heel, bloodstained tyranny, free peoples of the world, stand shoulder to shoulder*—one often has a curious feeling that one is not watching a live human being but some kind of dummy: a feeling which suddenly becomes stronger at moments when the light catches the speaker's spectacles and turns them into blank discs which seem to have no eyes behind them. And this is not altogether fanciful. A speaker who uses that kind of phraseology has gone some distance toward turning himself into a machine. The appropriate noises are coming out of his larynx, but his brain is not involved as it would be if he were choosing his words for himself. If the speech he is making is one that he is accustomed to make over and over again, he may be almost unconscious of what he is saying, as one is when one utters the responses in church. And this reduced state of consciousness, if not indispensable, is at any rate favorable to political conformity.

In our time, political speech and writing are largely the 16 defence of the indefensible. Things like the continuance of British rule in India, the Russian purges and deportations, the dropping of the atom bombs on Japan, can indeed be defended, but only by arguments which are too brutal for most people to face, and which do not square with the professed aims of political parties. Thus political language has to consist largely of euphemism, question-begging and sheer cloudy vagueness. Defenceless villages are bombarded from the air, the inhabitants driven out into the countryside, the cattle machine-gunned, the huts set on fire with incendiary bullets: this is called *pacification*. Millions of peasants are robbed of their farms and sent trudging along the roads with no more than they can carry: this is called *transfer of population* or *rectification of frontiers*. People are imprisoned for years without trial, or shot in the back of the neck or sent to die of scurvy in Arctic lumber camps: this is called *elimination of unreliable elements*. Such phraseology is needed if one wants to name things without calling up mental pictures of them. Consider for instance some comfortable English professor defending Russian totalitarianism. He cannot say outright, "I believe in killing off your opponents when you can get good results by doing so." Probably, therefore, he will say something like this:

"While freely conceding that the Soviet régime exhibits certain 17 features which the humanitarian may be inclined to deplore, we must, I think, agree that a certain curtailment of the right to political opposition is an unavoidable concomitant of transitional periods, and that the rigors which the Russian people have been called upon to undergo have been amply justified in the sphere of concrete achievement."

The inflated style itself is a kind of euphemism. A mass of 18 Latin words falls upon the facts like soft snow, blurring the outlines and covering up all the details. The great enemy of clear language is insincerity. When there is a gap between one's real and one's declared aims, one turns as it were instinctively to long words and exhausted idioms, like a cuttlefish squirting out ink. In our age there is no such thing as "keeping out of politics." All issues are political issues, and politics itself is a mass of lies, evasions, folly, hatred, and schizophrenia. When the general atmosphere is bad, language must suffer. I should expect to find—this is a guess which I have not sufficient knowledge to verify—that the German, Russian and Italian languages have all deteriorated in the last ten or fifteen years, as a result of dictatorship.

But if thought corrupts language, language can also corrupt 19 thought. A bad usage can spread by tradition and imitation, even among people who should and do know better. The debased language that I have been discussing is in some ways very convenient. Phrases like *a not unjustifiable assumption, leaves much to be desired, would serve no good purpose, a consideration which we should do well to bear in mind,* are a continuous temptation, a packet of aspirins always at one's elbow. Look back through this essay, and for certain you will find that I have again and again committed the very faults I am protesting against. By this morning's post I have received a pamphlet dealing with conditions in Germany. The author tells me that he "felt impelled" to write it. I open it at random, and here is almost the first sentence I see: "[The Allies] have an opportunity not only of achieving a radical transformation of Germany's social and political structure in such a way as to avoid a nationalistic reaction in Germany itself, but at the same time of laying the foundations of a co-operative and unified Europe." You see, he "feels impelled" to write—feels, presumably, that he has something new to say—and yet his words, like cavalry horses answering the bugle, group themselves automatically into the familiar dreary pattern. This invasion of one's mind by ready-made phrases *(lay the foundations, achieve a radical transformation)* can only be prevented if one is constantly on guard against them, and every such phrase anaesthetizes a portion of one's brain.

I said earlier that the decadence of our language is probably 20 curable. Those who deny this would argue, if they produced an argument at all, that language merely reflects existing social conditions, and that we cannot influence its development by any direct tinkering with words and constructions. So far as the general tone or spirit of a language goes, this may be true, but it is not true in detail. Silly words and expressions have often disappeared, not through any evolutionary process but owing to the conscious action of a minority. Two recent examples were *explore every avenue* and *leave no stone unturned*, which were killed by the jeers of a few journalists. There is a long list of flyblown metaphors which could similarly be got rid of if enough people would interest themselves in the job; and it should also be possible to laugh the *not un-* formation out of existence,[3] to reduce the amount of Latin and Greek in the average sentence, to drive out foreign phrases and strayed scientific words, and, in general, to make pretentiousness unfashionable. But all these are minor points. The defence of the English language implies more than this, and perhaps it is best to start by saying what it does *not* imply.

To begin with it has nothing to do with archaism, with the salvaging of obsolete words and turns of speech, or with the setting up of a "standard English" which must never be departed from. On the contrary, it is especially concerned with the scrapping of every word or idiom which has outworn its usefulness. It has nothing to do with correct grammar and syntax, which are of no importance so long as one makes one's meaning clear, or with the avoidance of Americanisms, or with having what is called a "good prose style." On the other hand, it is not concerned with fake simplicity and the attempt to make written English colloquial. Nor does it even imply in every case preferring the Saxon word to the Latin one, though it does imply using the fewest and shortest words that will cover one's meaning. What is above all needed is to let the meaning choose the word, and not the other way about. In prose, the worst thing one can do with words is to surrender to them. When you think of a concrete object, you think wordlessly, and then, if you want to describe the thing you have been visualizing you probably hunt about till you find the exact words that seem to fit it. When you think of something abstract you are more inclined to use words from the start, and unless you make a conscious effort to prevent it, the existing dialect will come rushing in and do the job for you, at the

21

---

[3] [Orwell's note] One can cure oneself of the *not un-* formation by memorizing this sentence: *A not unblack dog was chasing a not unsmall rabbit across a not ungreen field.*

expense of blurring or even changing your meaning. Probably it is better to put off using words as long as possible and get one's meaning as clear as one can through pictures and sensations. Afterwards one can choose—not simply *accept*—the phrases that will best cover the meaning, and then switch round and decide what impressions one's words are likely to make on another person. This last effort of the mind cuts out all stale or mixed images, all prefabricated phrases, needless repetitions, and humbug and vagueness generally. But one can often be in doubt about the effect of a word or a phrase, and one needs rules that one can rely on when instinct fails. I think the following rules will cover most cases:

(i) Never use a metaphor, simile or other figure of speech which you are used to seeing in print.
(ii) Never use a long word where a short one will do.
(iii) If it is possible to cut a word out, always cut it out.
(iv) Never use the passive where you can use the active.
(v) Never use a foreign phrase, a scientific word or a jargon word if you can think of an everyday English equivalent.
(vi) Break any of these rules sooner than say anything outright barbarous.

These rules sound elementary, and so they are, but they demand a deep change of attitude in anyone who has grown used to writing in the style now fashionable. One could keep all of them and still write bad English, but one could not write the kind of stuff that I quoted in those five specimens at the beginning of this article.

I have not here been considering the literary use of language, 22 but merely language as an instrument for expressing and not for concealing or preventing thought. Stuart Chase and others have come near to claiming that all abstract words are meaningless, and have used this as a pretext for advocating a kind of political quietism. Since you don't know what Fascism is, how can you struggle against Fascism? One need not swallow such absurdities as this, but one ought to recognize that the present political chaos is connected with the decay of language, and that one can probably bring about some improvement by starting at the verbal end. If you simplify your English, you are freed from the worst follies of orthodoxy. You cannot speak any of the necessary dialects, and when you make a stupid remark its stupidity will be obvious, even to yourself. Political language—and with variations this is true of all political parties, from Conservatives to Anarchists —is designed to make lies sound truthful and murder respectable, and to give an appearance of solidity to pure wind. One cannot change this all in a moment, but one can at least change one's own habits, and from time to time one can even, if one jeers loudly enough, send some worn-out and useless phrase—some *jackboot, Achilles' heel, hotbed, melting pot, acid test, veritable inferno,* or other lump of verbal refuse—into the dustbin where it belongs.

David Suzuki

■ ■ ■

The Pain of Animals

Dr. David Suzuki (b. 1936), geneticist, writer, broadcaster, environmentalist, was born in Vancouver, spent part of his childhood in a B.C. internment camp during World War Two, and grew up in London, Ontario. Educated at Amherst College and the University of Chicago (PhD 1961), Suzuki joined the University of British Columbia in 1963, where he is a professor in the Department of Zoology. Wanting to increase public awareness both of science itself and of the issues arising from it, Suzuki began his career as a broadcaster in 1971 as host of the TV series *Suzuki on Science*. Since then he has become one of Canada's most recognizable public figures. A Fellow of the Royal Society of Canada and an Officer of the Order of Canada, Suzuki has been the recipient of many awards for outstanding academic contributions (a partial list includes twelve honorary degrees, and medals from the Science Council of B.C., the Biological Council of Canada, the UN Environment Program, and the Canadian Medical Association); for broadcasting (two Gemini Awards); and for writing (UNESCO Kalinga Prize for science). Suzuki currently hosts the long-running TV series *The Nature of Things*. His books include *Metamorphosis: Stages in a Life* (1987), *Genethics: The Ethics of Engineering Genes* (1988), *It's a Matter of Survival* (1990), *Wisdom of the Elders* (1992), and *An Introduction to Genetic Analysis*, 5th ed. (1993). *Inventing the Future* (1989), from which the following essay is reprinted, is a collection of some of the weekly columns Suzuki wrote in the 1980s for the *Toronto Star* and later *The Globe and Mail*. This essay first appeared in *The Globe* on June 4, 1988.

■

Medical technology has taken us beyond the normal barriers 1 of life and death and thereby created unprecedented choices in *human* lives. Until recently, we have taken for granted our right to use other species in any way we see fit. Food, clothing, muscle power have been a few of the benefits we've derived from this exploitation. This tradition has continued into scientific research where animals are studied and "sacrificed" for human benefit. Now serious questions are being asked about our right to do this.

Modern biological research is based on a shared evolutionary 2 history of organisms that enables us to extrapolate from one organism to another. Thus, most fundamental concepts in heredity were first shown in fruit flies, molecular genetics began using bacteria and viruses and much of physiology and psychology has been based on studies in mice and rats. But today, as extinction rates have multiplied as a result of human activity, we have begun to ask what right we have to use all other animate forms simply to increase human knowledge or for profit or entertainment. Underlying the "animal rights" movement is the troubling question of where we fit in the rest of the natural world.

When I was young, one of my prized possessions was a BB 3 gun. Dad taught me how to use it safely and I spent many hours wandering through the woods in search of prey. It's not easy to get close enough to a wild animal to kill it with a BB gun, but I did hit a few pigeons and starlings. I ate everything I shot. Then as a teenager, I graduated to a .22 rifle and with it, I killed rabbits and even shot a pheasant once.

One year I saw an ad for a metal slingshot in a comic book. I 4 ordered it, and when it arrived, I practised for weeks shooting marbles at a target. I got to be a pretty good shot and decided to go after something live. Off I went to the woods and soon spotted a squirrel minding its own business doing whatever squirrels do. I gave chase and began peppering marbles at it until finally it jumped onto a tree, ran to the top and found itself trapped. I kept blasting away and grazed it a couple of times so it was only a matter of time before I would knock it down. Suddenly, the squirrel began to cry—a piercing shriek of terror and anguish. That animal's wail shook me to the core and I was overwhelmed with horror and shame at what I was doing—for no other reason than conceit with my prowess with a slingshot, I was going to *kill* another being. I threw away the slingshot and my guns and have never hunted again.

All my life, I have been an avid fisherman. Fish have always 5 been the main source of meat protein in my family, and I have never considered fishing a sport. But there is no denying that it is exciting to reel in a struggling fish. We call it "playing" the fish, as if the wild animal's desperate struggle for survival is some kind of game.

I did "pleasure-fish" once while filming for a television report 6 on the science of fly fishing. We fished a famous trout stream in the Catskill Mountains of New York state where all fish had to be caught and released. The fish I caught had mouths gouged and pocked by previous encounters with hooks. I found no pleasure in it because to me fish are to be caught for consumption. Today, I continue to fish for food, but I do so with a profound awareness that I am a predator of animals possessing well-developed nervous systems that detect pain. Fishing and hunting have forced me to confront the way we exploit other animals.

I studied the genetics of fruit flies for twenty-five years and during that time probably raised and killed tens of millions of them without a thought. In the early seventies, my lab discovered a series of mutations affecting behaviour of flies, and this find led us into an investigation of nerves and muscles. I applied for and received research funds to study behaviour in flies on the basis of the *similarity* of their neuromuscular systems to ours. In fact, psychologists and neurobiologists analyse behaviour, physiology and neuroanatomy of guinea pigs, rats, mice and other animals as *models* for human behaviour. So our nervous systems must closely resemble those of other mammals.   7

These personal anecdotes raise uncomfortable questions. What gives us the right to exploit other living organisms as we see fit? How do we know that these other creatures don't feel pain or anguish just as we do? Perhaps there's no problem with fruit flies, but where do we draw the line? I used to rationalize angling because fish are cold-blooded, as if warm-bloodedness indicates some kind of demarcation of brain development or greater sensitivity to pain. But anyone who has watched a fish's frantic fight to escape knows that it exhibits all the manifestations of pain and fear.   8

I've been thinking about these questions again after spending a weekend in the Queen Charlotte Islands watching grey whales close up. The majesty and freedom of these magnificent mammals contrasted strikingly with the appearance of whales imprisoned in aquariums. Currently, the Vancouver Public Aquarium is building a bigger pool for some of its whales. In a radio interview, an aquarium representative was asked whether even the biggest pool can be adequate for animals that normally have the entire ocean to rove. Part of her answer was that if we watched porpoises in the pool, we'd see that "they are quite happy."   9

That woman was projecting human perceptions and emotions on the porpoises. Our ability to empathize with other people and living things is one of our endearing qualities. Just watch someone with a beloved pet, an avid gardener with plants or, for that matter, even an owner of a new car and you will see how readily we can personalize and identify with another living organism   10 or an object. But are we justified in our inferences about captive animals in their cages?

Most wild animals have evolved with a built-in need to move 11
freely over vast distances, fly in the air or swim through the ocean. Can a wild animal imprisoned in a small cage or pool, removed from its habitat and forced to conform to the impositions of our demands, ever be considered "happy"?

Animal rights activists are questioning our right to exploit 12
animals, especially in scientific research. Scientists are understandably defensive, especially after labs have been broken into, experiments ruined and animals "liberated." But just as I have had to question my hunting and fishing, scientists cannot avoid confronting the issues raised, especially in relation to our closest relatives, the primates.

People love to watch monkeys in a circus or zoo and a great 13
deal of the amusement comes from the recognition of ourselves in them. But our relationship with them is closer than just superficial similarities. When doctors at Loma Linda hospital in California implanted the heart of a baboon into the chest of Baby Fae, they were exploiting our close *biological* relationship.

Any reports on experimentation with familiar mammals like 14
cats and dogs are sure to raise alarm among the lay public. But the use of primates is most controversial. In September 1987, at the Wildlife Film Festival in Bath, England, I watched a film shot on December 7, 1986, by a group of animal liberationists who had broken into SEMA, a biomedical research facility in Maryland. It was such a horrifying document that many in the audience rushed out after a few minutes. There were many scenes that I could not watch. As the intruders entered the facility, the camera followed to peer past cage doors, opened to reveal the animals inside. I am not ashamed to admit that I wept as baby monkeys deprived of any contact with other animals seized the fingers of their liberators and clung to them as our babies would to us. Older animals cowered in their tiny prisons, shaking from fear at the sudden appearance of people.

The famous chimpanzee expert, Jane Goodall, also screened 15
the same film and as a result asked for permission to visit the SEMA facility. This is what she saw (*American Scientist*, November-December 1987):

> Room after room was lined with small, bare cages, stacked one above the other, in which monkeys circled round and round and chimpanzees sat huddled, far gone in depression and despair.

Young chimpanzees, three or four years old, were crammed, two together into tiny cages measuring 57 cm by 57 cm and only 61 cm high. They could hardly turn around. Not yet part of any experiment, they had been confined to these cages for more than three months.

The chimps had each other for comfort, but they would not remain together for long. Once they are infected, probably with hepatitis, they will be separated and placed in another cage. And there they will remain, living in conditions of severe sensory deprivation, for the next several years. During that time they will become insane.

Goodall's horror sprang from an intimate knowledge of 16 chimpanzees in their native habitat. There, she has learned, chimps are nothing like the captive animals that we know. In the wild, they are highly social, requiring constant interaction and physical contact. They travel long distances, and they rest in soft beds they make in the trees. Laboratory cages do not provide the conditions needed to fulfill the needs of these social, emotional and highly intelligent animals.

Ian Redmond (*BBC Wildlife*, April 1988) gives us a way to 17 understand the horror of what lab conditions do to chimps:

Imagine locking a two- or three-year-old child in a metal box the size of an isolette—solid walls, floor and ceiling, and a glass door that clamps shut, blotting out most external sounds—and then leaving him or her for months, the only contact, apart from feeding, being when the door swings open and masked figures reach in and take samples of blood or tissue before shoving him back and clamping the door shut again. Over the past 10 years, 94 young chimps at SEMA have endured this procedure.

Chimpanzees, along with the gorilla, are our closest relatives, 18 sharing ninety-nine per cent of our genes. And it's that biological proximity that makes them so useful for research—we can try out experiments, study infections and test vaccines on them as models for people. And although there are only about 40,000 chimps left in the wild, compared to millions a few decades ago, the scientific demand for more has increased with the discovery of AIDS.

No chimpanzee has ever contracted AIDS, but the virus 19 grows in them, so scientists argue that chimps will be invaluable for testing vaccines. On February 19, 1988, the National Institute of Health in the U.S. co-sponsored a meeting to discuss the use of chimpanzees in research. Dr. Maurice Hilleman, Director of the Merck Institute for Therapeutic Research, reported:

We need more chimps. . . . The chimpanzee is certainly a
threatened species and there have been bans on importing the
animal into the United States and into other countries, even
though . . . the chimpanzee is considered to be an agricultural
pest in many parts of the world where it exists. And secondly,
it's being destroyed by virtue of environmental encroachment—
that is, destroying the natural habitat. So these chimpanzees
are being eliminated by virtue of their being an agricultural
pest and by the fact that their habitat is being destroyed. So
why not rescue them? The number of chimpanzees for AIDS
research in the United States [is] somewhere in the hundreds
and certainly, we need thousands.

Our capacity to rationalize our behaviour and needs is 20
remarkable. Chimpanzees have occupied their niche over tens
of millennia of biological evolution. *We* are newcomers who have
encroached on *their* territory, yet by defining them as *pests* we
render them expendable. As Redmond says, "The fact that the
chimpanzee is our nearest zoological relative makes it perhaps the
unluckiest animal on earth, because what the kinship has come to
mean is that we feel free to do most of the things to a chimp that
we mercifully refrain from doing to each other."

And so the impending epidemic of AIDS confronts us not 21
only with our inhumanity to each other but to other species.

Jonathan Swift

■■■

A Modest Proposal

Jonathan Swift (1667–1745), political and social satirist, essayist, and poet, was born in Ireland of English parents. Taking his MA from Oxford in 1692 and becoming ordained as a priest in the Church of Ireland (the Irish branch of the Anglican Church) in 1695, Swift became Dean of St. Patrick's Cathedral in Dublin in 1713. Swift was acquainted with and often close to the major political figures of the day and wrote influential political tracts both in England and in Ireland, between which countries he split his time early in his career. He spent most of his later years in Ireland, becoming increasingly distressed and incensed by political and economic conditions there. *A Modest Proposal* is one of a number of pamphlets speaking to these conditions. Published in 1729 and circulated in Dublin, it was reprinted immediately in London, and appeared not only in three separate London editions in 1730 but also in several subsequent collections in both cities. It has been reprinted and collected many times since then, and, along with *Gulliver's Travels* (1726), is perhaps Swift's best-known work.

A MODEST PROPOSAL FOR

Preventing the Children of poor People in Ireland,
from being a Burden to their Parents or Country;
and for making them beneficial to the Publick.

Written in the Year 1729

IT is a melancholly Object to those, who walk through this great   1
Town, or travel in the Country; when they see the *Streets,* the *Roads,* and *Cabbin-doors* crowded with *Beggars* of the Female Sex, followed by three, four, or six Children, *all in Rags,* and importuning every Passenger for an Alms. These *Mothers,* instead of being able to work for their honest Livelihood, are forced to employ all their Time in stroling to beg Sustenance for their *helpless Infants;* who, as they grow up, either turn *Thieves* for want of Work;

or leave their *dear Native Country, to fight for the Pretender in* Spain, or sell themselves to the *Barbadoes.*

I THINK it is agreed by all Parties, that this prodigious Number 2 of Children in the Arms, or on the Backs, or at the *Heels* of their *Mothers,* and frequently of their *Fathers,* is *in the present deplorable State of the Kingdom,* a very great additional Grievance; and therefore, whoever could find out a fair, cheap, and easy Method of making these Children sound and useful Members of the Commonwealth, would deserve so well of the Publick, as to have his Statue set up for a Preserver of the Nation.

BUT my Intention is very far from being confined to provide 3 only for the Children of *professed Beggars:* It is of a much greater Extent, and shall take in the whole Number of Infants at a certain Age, who are born of Parents, in effect as little able to support them, as those who demand our Charity in the Streets.

As to my own Part, having turned my Thoughts for many 4 Years, upon this important Subject, and maturely weighed the several *Schemes of other Projectors,* I have always found them grosly mistaken in their Computation. It is true a Child, *just dropt from its Dam,* may be supported by her Milk, for a Solar Year with little other Nourishment; at most not above the Value of two Shillings; which the Mother may certainly get, or the Value in *Scraps,* by her lawful Occupation of *Begging:* And, it is exactly at one Year old, that I propose to provide for them in such a Manner, as, instead of being a Charge upon their *Parents,* or the *Parish,* or *wanting Food and Raiment* for the rest of their Lives; they shall, on the contrary, contribute to the Feeding, and partly to the Cloathing, of many Thousands.

THERE is likewise another great Advantage in my *Scheme,* that 5 it will prevent those *voluntary Abortions,* and that horrid Practice of *Women murdering their Bastard Children;* alas! too frequent among us; sacrificing the *poor innocent Babes,* I doubt, more to avoid the Expence than the Shame; which would move Tears and Pity in the most Savage and inhuman Breast.

THE Number of Souls in *Ireland* being usually reckoned one 6 Million and a half; of these I calculate there may be about Two hundred Thousand Couple whose Wives are Breeders; from which Number I subtract thirty thousand Couples, who are able to maintain their own Children; although I apprehend there cannot be so many, under *the present Distresses of the Kingdom;* but this being granted, there will remain an Hundred and Seventy Thousand Breeders. I again subtract Fifty Thousand, for those

Women who miscarry, or whose Children die by Accident, or Disease, within the Year. There only remain an Hundred and Twenty Thousand Children of poor Parents, annually born: The Question therefore is, How this Number shall be reared, and provided for? Which, as I have already said, under the present Situation of Affairs, is utterly impossible, by all the Methods hitherto proposed: For we *can neither employ them in Handicraft* or *Agriculture;* we neither build Houses, (I mean in the Country) nor cultivate Land: They can very seldom pick up a Livelyhood *by Stealing* until they arrive at six Years old; except where they are of towardly Parts; although, I confess, they learn the Rudiments much earlier; during which Time, they can, however, be properly looked upon only as *Probationers;* as I have been informed by a principal Gentleman in the County of *Cavan*, who protested to me, that he never knew above one or two Instances under the Age of six, even in a Part of the Kingdom *so renowned for the quickest Proficiency in that Art.*

I AM assured by our Merchants, that a Boy or a Girl before 7 twelve Years old, is no saleable Commodity; and even when they come to this Age, they will not yield above Three Pounds, or Three Pounds and half a Crown at most, on the Exchange; which cannot turn to Account either to the Parents or the Kingdom; the Charge of Nutriment and Rags, having been at least four Times that Value.

I SHALL now therefore humbly propose my own Thoughts; 8 which I hope will not be liable to the least Objection.

I HAVE been assured by a very knowing American of my 9 Acquaintance in *London;* that a young healthy Child, well nursed, is, at a Year old, a most delicious, nourishing, and wholesome Food; whether *Stewed, Roasted, Baked,* or *Boiled;* and, I make no doubt, that it will equally serve in a *Fricasie,* or *Ragoust.*

I DO therefore humbly offer it to *publick Consideration,* that of 10 the Hundred and Twenty Thousand Children, already computed, Twenty thousand may be reserved for Breed; whereof only one Fourth Part to be Males; which is more than we allow to *Sheep, black Cattle,* or *Swine;* and my Reason is, that these Children are seldom the Fruits of Marriage, *a Circumstance not much regarded by our Savages;* therefore, *one Male* will be sufficient to serve *four Females.* That the remaining Hundred thousand, may, at a Year old, be offered in Sale to the *Persons of Quality* and *Fortune,* through the Kingdom; always advising the Mother to let them suck plentifully in the last Month, so as to render them plump, and fat for a good Table. A Child will make two Dishes at an Entertainment for Friends; and when the Family dines alone, the fore or hind Quarter will make a reasonable Dish; and seasoned with a little Pepper or Salt, will be very good Boiled on the fourth Day, especially in *Winter*.

I HAVE reckoned upon a Medium, that a Child just born will   11
weigh Twelve Pounds; and in a solar Year, if tolerably nursed, encreaseth to twenty eight Pounds.

I GRANT this Food will be somewhat dear, and therefore very   12
proper for Landlords; who, as they have already devoured most of the Parents, seem to have the best Title to the Children.

INFANTS Flesh will be in Season throughout the Year; but more   13
plentiful in *March*, and a little before and after: For we are told by a grave* Author, an eminent *French* Physician, that *Fish being a prolifick Dyet*, there are more Children born in *Roman Catholick Countries* about Nine Months after *Lent*, than at any other Season: Therefore reckoning a Year after *Lent*, the Markets will be more glutted than usual; because the Number of *Popish Infants*, is, at least, three to one in this Kingdom; and therefore it will have one other Collateral Advantage, by lessening the Number of *Papists* among us.

I HAVE already computed the Charge of nursing a Beggar's   14
Child (in which List I reckon all *Cottagers, Labourers,* and Four fifths of the *Farmers)* to be about two Shillings *per Annum*, Rags included; and I believe, no Gentleman would repine to give Ten Shillings for the *Carcase of a good fat Child;* which, as I have said, will make four Dishes of excellent nutritive Meat, when he hath only some particular Friend, or his own Family, to dine with him. Thus the Squire will learn to be a good Landlord, and grow popular among his Tenants; the Mother will have Eight Shillings net Profit, and be fit for Work until she produceth another Child.

THOSE who are more thrifty *(as I must confess the Times require)*   15
may flay the Carcase; the Skin of which, artificially dressed, will make admirable *Gloves for Ladies,* and *Summer Boots for fine Gentlemen.*

As to our City of *Dublin;* Shambles may be appointed for this   16
Purpose, in the most convenient Parts of it; and Butchers we may be assured will not be wanting; although I rather recommend buying the Children alive, and dressing them hot from the Knife, as we do *roasting Pigs.*

*Rabelais

A VERY worthy Person, *a true Lover of his Country,* and whose   17
Virtues I highly esteem, was lately pleased, in discoursing on
this Matter, to offer a Refinement upon my Scheme. He said, that
many Gentlemen of this Kingdom, having of late destroyed their
Deer; he conceived, that the Want of Venison might be well
supplied by the Bodies of young Lads and Maidens, not exceeding
fourteen Years of Age, nor under twelve; so great a Number of
both Sexes in every County being now ready to starve, for Want
of Work and Service: And these to be disposed of by their Parents,
if alive, or otherwise by their nearest Relations. But with due
Deference to so excellent a Friend, and so deserving a Patriot, I
cannot be altogether in his Sentiments. For as to the Males, my
American Acquaintance assured me from frequent Experience,
that their Flesh was generally tough and lean, like that of our
School-boys, by continual Exercise, and their Taste disagreeable;
and to fatten them would not answer the Charge. Then, as to the
Females, it would, I think, with humble Submission, *be a Loss to
the Publick,* because they soon would become Breeders themselves:
And besides it is not improbable, that some scrupulous People
might be apt to censure such a Practice (although indeed very
unjustly) as a little bordering upon Cruelty; which, I confess,
hath always been with me the strongest Objection against any
Project, how well soever intended.

BUT in order to justify my Friend; he confessed, that this   18
Expedient was put into his Head by the famous *Salmanaazor,* a
Native of the Island *Formosa,* who came from thence to *London,*
above twenty Years ago, and in Conversation told my Friend,
that in his Country, when any young Person happened to be put
to Death, the Executioner sold the Carcase to *Persons of Quality,* as
a prime Dainty; and that, in his Time, the Body of a plump Girl
of fifteen, who was crucified for an Attempt to poison the
Emperor, was sold to his Imperial *Majesty's prime Minister of State,*
and other great *Mandarins* of the Court, *in Joints from the Gibbet,* at
Four hundred Crowns. Neither indeed can I deny, that if the
same Use were made of several plump young girls in this Town,
who, without one single Groat to their Fortunes, cannot stir
Abroad without a Chair, and appear at the *Play-house,* and
Assemblies in foreign Fineries, which they never will pay for; the
Kingdom would not be the worse.

SOME Persons of a desponding Spirit are in great Concern   19
about that vast Number of poor People, who are Aged, Diseased,
or Maimed; and I have been desired to employ my Thoughts

what Course may be taken, to ease the Nation of so grievous an Incumbrance. But I am not in the least Pain upon that Matter; because it is very well known, that they are every Day *dying,* and *rotting,* by *Cold* and *Famine,* and *Filth,* and *Vermin,* as fast as can be reasonably expected. And as to the younger Labourers, they are now in almost as hopeful a Condition: They cannot get Work, and consequently pine away for Want of Nourishment, to a Degree, that if at any Time they are accidentally hired to common Labour, they have not Strength to perform it; and thus the Country, and themselves, are in a fair Way of being soon delivered from the Evils to come.

I HAVE too long digressed; and therefore shall return to my   20
Subject. I think the Advantages by the Proposal which I have made, are obvious, and many, as well as of the highest Importance.

FOR, *First,* as I have already observed, it would greatly lessen   21
the *Number of Papists,* with whom we are yearly overrun; being the principal Breeders of the Nation, as well as our most dangerous Enemies; and who stay at home on Purpose, with a Design to *deliver the Kingdom to the Pretender;* hoping to take their Advantage by the Absence *of so many good Protestants,* who have chosen rather to leave their Country, than stay at home, and pay Tithes against their Conscience, to an idolatrous *Episcopal Curate.*

SECONDLY, The poorer Tenants will have something valuable   22
of their own, which, by Law, may be made liable to Distress, and help to pay their Landlord's Rent; their Corn and Cattle being already seized, and *Money a Thing unknown.*

THIRDLY, Whereas the Maintenance of an Hundred Thousand   23
Children, from two Years old, and upwards, cannot be computed at less than ten Shillings a Piece *per Annum,* the Nation's Stock will be thereby encreased Fifty Thousand Pounds *per Annum;* besides the Profit of a new Dish, introduced to the Tables of all *Gentlemen of Fortune* in the Kingdom, who have any Refinement in Taste; and the Money will circulate among ourselves, the Goods being entirely of our own Growth and Manufacture.

FOURTHLY, The constant Breeders, besides the Gain of Eight   24
Shillings *Sterling per Annum,* by the Sale of their Children, will be rid of the Charge of maintaining them after the first Year.

FIFTHLY, This Food would likewise bring great *Custom to*   25
Taverns, where the Vintners will certainly be so prudent, as to procure the best Receipts for dressing it to Perfection; and consequently, have their Houses frequented by all the *fine Gentlemen,* who justly value themselves upon their Knowledge

in good Eating; and a skilful Cook, who understands how to oblige his Guests, will contrive to make it as expensive as they please.

SIXTHLY, This would be a great Inducement to Marriage, which 26 all wise Nations have either encouraged by Rewards, or enforced by Laws and Penalties. It would encrease the Care and Tenderness of Mothers towards their Children, when they were sure of a Settlement for Life, to the poor Babes, provided in some Sort by the Publick, to their annual Profit instead of Expence. We should soon see an honest Emulation among the married Women, *which of them could bring the fattest Child to the Market.* Men would become as *fond* of their Wives, during the Time of their Pregnancy, as they are now of their *Mares* in Foal, their *Cows* in Calf, or *Sows* when they are ready to farrow; nor offer to beat or kick them, (as it is too *frequent* a Practice) for fear of a Miscarriage.

MANY other Advantages might be enumerated. For instance, 27 the Addition of some Thousand Carcasses in our Exportation of barrelled Beef: The Propagation of *Swines Flesh,* and Improvement in the Art of making good *Bacon;* so much wanted among us by the great Destruction of *Pigs,* too frequent at our Tables, and are no way comparable in Taste, or Magnificence, to a well-grown fat yearling Child; which, roasted whole, will make a considerable Figure at a *Lord Mayor's Feast,* or any other publick Entertainment. But this, and many others, I omit; being studious of Brevity.

SUPPOSING that one Thousand Families in this City, would be 28 constant Customers for Infants Flesh; besides others who might have it at *merry Meetings,* particularly *Weddings* and *Christenings;* I compute that *Dublin* would take off, annually, about Twenty Thousand Carcasses; and the rest of the Kingdom (where probably they will be sold somewhat cheaper) the remaining Eighty Thousand.

→ I CAN think of no one Objection, that will possibly be raised 29 against this Proposal; unless it should be urged, that the Number of People will be thereby much lessened in the Kingdom. This I freely own; and it was indeed one principal Design in offering it to the World. I desire the Reader will observe, that I calculate my Remedy *for this one individual Kingdom of* IRELAND, *and for no other that ever was, is, or I think ever can be upon Earth.* Therefore, let no man talk to me of other Expedients: *Of taxing our Absentees at five Shillings a Pound: Of using neither Cloaths, nor Houshold Furniture except what is of our own Growth and Manufacture: Of utterly rejecting the Materials and Instruments that promote foreign Luxury: Of curing the Expensiveness of Pride, Vanity, Idleness, and*

*Gaming in our Women: Of introducing a Vein of Parsimony, Prudence
and Temperance: Of learning to love our Country, wherein we differ
even from* LAPLANDERS, *and the Inhabitants of* TOPINAMBOO: *Of quitting
our Animosities, and Factions; nor act any longer like the* Jews, *who
were murdering one another at the very Moment their City was taken:
Of being a little cautious not to sell our Country and Consciences for
nothing: Of teaching Landlords to have, at least, one Degree of Mercy
towards their Tenants.* Lastly, *Of putting a Spirit of Honesty, Industry,
and Skill into our Shop-keepers; who, if a Resolution could now be
taken to buy only our native Goods, would immediately unite to cheat
and exact upon us in the Price, the Measure, and the Goodness; nor
could ever yet be brought to make one fair Proposal of just Dealing,
though often and earnestly invited to it.*

THEREFORE I repeat, let no Man talk to me of these and the like   30
Expedients; till he hath at least, a Glimpse of Hope, that there will
ever be some hearty and sincere Attempt to put *them in Practice.*

BUT, as to my self; having been wearied out for many Years   31
with offering vain, idle, visionary Thoughts; and at length utterly
despairing of Success, I fortunately fell upon this Proposal; which,
as it is wholly new, so it hath something *solid* and *real,* of no
Expence, and little Trouble, full in our own Power; and whereby
we can incur no Danger in *disobliging* ENGLAND: For, this Kind of
Commodity will not bear Exportation; the Flesh being of too
tender a Consistence, to admit a long Continuance in Salt;
*although, perhaps, I could name a Country, which would be glad to eat
up our whole Nation without it.*

AFTER all, I am not so violently bent upon my own Opinion,   32
as to reject any Offer proposed by wise Men, which shall be found
equally innocent, cheap, easy, and effectual. But before something
of that Kind shall be advanced, in Contradiction to my Scheme,
and offering a better; I desire the Author, or Authors, will be
pleased maturely to consider two Points. *First,* As Things now
stand, how they will be able to find Food and Raiment, for a
Hundred Thousand useless Mouths and Backs? And *secondly,*
There being a round Million of Creatures in human Figure,
throughout this Kingdom; whose whole Subsistence, put into a
common Stock, would leave them in Debt two Millions of Pounds
Sterling; adding those, who are Beggars by Profession, to the Bulk
of Farmers, Cottagers, and Labourers, with their Wives and
Children, who are Beggars in Effect; I desire those Politicians,
who dislike my Overture, and may perhaps be so bold to attempt
an Answer, that they will first ask the Parents of these Mortals,

Whether they would not, at this Day, think it a great Happiness to have been sold for Food at a Year old, in the Manner I prescribe; and thereby have avoided such a perpetual Scene of Misfortunes, as they have since gone through; by the *Oppression of Landlords;* the Impossibility of paying Rent, without Money or Trade; the Want of common Sustenance, with neither House nor Cloaths, to cover them from the Inclemencies of Weather; and the most inevitable Prospect of intailing the like, or greater Miseries upon their Breed for ever.

I PROFESS, in the Sincerity of my Heart, that I have not the least 33 personal Interest, in endeavouring to promote this necessary Work; having no other Motive than the *publick Good of my country, by advancing our Trade, providing for Infants, relieving the Poor, and giving some Pleasure to the Rich.* I have no Children, by which I can propose to get a single Penny; the youngest being nine Years old, and my Wife past Child-bearing.

Lewis Thomas

■■■

Notes on Punctuation

Lewis Thomas (1913–1993), physician, professor, and essayist, was born in Flushing, New York, and attended both Princeton University and Harvard Medical School, from which he graduated in 1937. His distinguished medical career included teaching and research at several of America's top universities; he was Dean of Medicine at New York University and Yale and Chancellor of the Memorial Sloan-Kettering Cancer Center in New York City. In 1971, after publishing many academic articles, Thomas began writing a monthly column entitled "Notes of a Biology Watcher" for the *New England Journal of Medicine.* Often exploring the relationship between humans and the worlds of biology and medicine, these columns also reveal an interest in language, culture, and the arts; and their graceful, lucid style has earned Thomas popular as well as academic acclaim. In 1974 his columns were collected and published as *The Lives of a Cell: Notes of a Biology Watcher,* which won a National Book Award. Other essay collections include *The Medusa and the Snail* (1979), *Late Night Thoughts on Listening to Mahler's Ninth Symphony* (1983), *Et Cetera, Et Cetera: Notes of a Word Watcher* (1990), and *The Fragile Species* (1992). The following essay comes from *The Medusa and the Snail.*

There are no precise rules about punctuation (Fowler lays out 1 some general advice (as best he can under the complex circumstances of English prose (he points out, for example, that we possess only four stops (the comma, the semicolon, the colon and the period (the question mark and exclamation point are not, strictly speaking, stops; they are indicators of tone (oddly enough, the Greeks employed the semicolon for their question mark (it produces a strange sensation to read a Greek sentence which is a straightforward question: Why weepest thou; (instead of Why weepest thou? (and, of course, there are parentheses (which are surely a kind of punctuation making this whole matter much more complicated by having to count up the left-handed parentheses in order to be sure of closing with the right number (but if the parentheses were left out, with nothing to work with but the stops, we would have considerably more flexibility in the deploying of layers of meaning than if we tried to separate all the clauses by physical barriers (and in the latter case, while we might have more precision and exactitude for our meaning, we would lose the essential flavor of language, which is its wonderful ambiguity)))))))))))).

The commas are the most useful and usable of all the stops. It is highly important to put them in place as you go along. If you try to come back after doing a paragraph and stick them in the various spots that tempt you you will discover that they tend to swarm like minnows into all sorts of crevices whose existence you hadn't realized and before you know it the whole long sentence becomes immobilized and lashed up squirming in commas. Better to use them sparingly, and with affection, precisely when the need for each one arises, nicely, by itself. 2

I have grown fond of semicolons in recent years. The semicolon tells you that there is still some question about the preceding full sentence; something needs to be added; it reminds you sometimes of the Greek usage. It is almost always a greater pleasure to come across a semicolon than a period. The period tells you that that is that; if you didn't get all the meaning you wanted or expected, anyway you got all the writer intended to parcel out and now you have to move along. But with a semicolon there you get a pleasant little feeling of expectancy; there is more to come; read on; it will get clearer. 3

Colons are a lot less attractive, for several reasons: firstly, they give you the feeling of being rather ordered around, or at least having your nose pointed in a direction you might not be inclined to take if left to yourself, and, secondly, you suspect you're in for one of those sentences that will be labeling the points to be made: firstly, secondly and so forth, with the implication that you haven't sense enough to keep track of a sequence of notions without having them numbered. Also, many writers use this system loosely and incompletely, starting out with number one and number two as though counting off on their fingers but then going on and on without the succession of labels you've been led to expect, leaving you floundering about searching for the ninethly or seventeenthly that ought to be there but isn't. 4

Exclamation points are the most irritating of all. Look! they say, look at what I just said! How amazing is my thought! It is like being forced to watch someone else's small child jumping up and down crazily in the center of the living room shouting to 5 attract attention. If a sentence really has something of importance to say, something quite remarkable, it doesn't need a mark to point it out. And if it is really, after all, a banal sentence needing more zing, the exclamation point simply emphasizes its banality!

Quotation marks should be used honestly and sparingly,   6
when there is a genuine quotation at hand, and it is necessary to be very rigorous about the words enclosed by the marks. If something is to be quoted, the *exact* words must be used. If part of it must be left out because of space limitations, it is good manners to insert three dots to indicate the omission, but it is unethical to do this if it means connecting two thoughts which the original author did not intend to have tied together. Above all, quotation marks should not be used for ideas that you'd like to disown, things in the air so to speak. Nor should they be put in place around clichés; if you want to use a cliché you must take full responsibility for it yourself and not try to fob it off on anon., or on society. The most objectionable misuse of quotation marks, but one which illustrates the dangers of misuse in ordinary prose, is seen in advertising, especially in advertisements for small restaurants, for example "just around the corner," or "a good place to eat." No single, identifiable, citable person ever really said, for the record, "just around the corner," much less "a good place to eat," least likely of all for restaurants of the type that use this type of prose.

The dash is a handy device, informal and essentially playful,   7
telling you that you're about to take off on a different tack but still in some way connected with the present course—only you have to remember that the dash is there, and either put a second dash at the end of the notion to let the reader know that he's back on course, or else end the sentence, as here, with a period.

The greatest danger in punctuation is for poetry. Here it is   8
necessary to be as economical and parsimonious with commas and periods as with the words themselves, and any marks that seem to carry their own subtle meanings, like dashes and little rows of periods, even semicolons and question marks, should be left out altogether rather than inserted to clog up the thing with ambiguity. A single exclamation point in a poem, no matter what else the poem has to say, is enough to destroy the whole work.

The things I like best in T. S. Eliot's poetry, especially in the   9
Four Quartets, are the semicolons. You cannot hear them, but they are there, laying out the connections between the images and the ideas. Sometimes you get a glimpse of a semicolon

coming, a few lines farther on, and it is like climbing a steep path through woods and seeing a wooden bench just at a bend in the road ahead, a place where you can expect to sit for a moment, catching your breath.

Commas can't do this sort of thing; they can only tell you   10 how the different parts of a complicated thought are to be fitted together, but you can't sit, not even take a breath, just because of a comma,

Henry David Thoreau

■ ■ ■

Civil Disobedience

Henry David Thoreau (1817–1862) was born in Concord, Massachusetts, and educated at Harvard University, where he studied a variety of subjects including the classics, philosophy, and modern languages. After graduating in 1837, Thoreau taught school for four years; thereafter, aspiring to become a writer, he worked at an assortment of odd jobs before moving to a small cabin on property owned by his friend, writer and philosopher Ralph Waldo Emerson, near Concord. During his sojourn at Walden Pond, from 1845–47, Thoreau put into practice the transcendentalist philosophical principles of self-reliance expounded by Emerson. The journal he kept of his life at the pond, *Walden, or, Life in the Woods* (1854), is one of his best-known works. The other is the essay "Civil Disobedience." Its genesis was the brief time—one day—Thoreau spent in jail in July 1846 for refusing to pay his poll tax. Although the tax was paid that evening, probably by his aunt, Thoreau wanted to use his incarceration as defiant act to protest slavery and the Mexican War, and insisted on spending the night in jail. Two years later, Thoreau delivered "Civil Disobedience" as a lecture to the Concord Lyceum (February, 1848); it was later published under the title "Resistance to Civil Government" in *Aesthetic Papers* (1849), a collection of essays edited by Elizabeth Peabody. After Thoreau's death it appeared under the title "Civil Disobedience" in *A Yankee In Canada, with Anti-slavery and Reform Papers* (1866). The essay had little impact when it was first published, but in the twentieth century, reformers and activists such as Mahatma Ghandhi and Martin Luther King have used Thoreau's ideas to develop the theory and practice of passive resistance.

■ _____ ■

I heartily accept the motto,—"That government is best which governs least;" and I should like to see it acted up to more rapidly and systematically. Carried out, it finally amounts to this, which also I believe,—"That government is best which governs not at all;" and when men are prepared for it, that will be the kind of government which they will have. Government is at best but an expedient; but most governments are usually, and all governments are sometimes, inexpedient. The objections which have been brought against a standing army, and they are many and weighty, and deserve to prevail, may also at last be brought against a standing government. The standing army is only an arm of the standing government. The government itself, which is only the mode which the people have chosen to execute their will, is equally liable to be abused and perverted before the people can act through it. Witness the present Mexican war, the work of comparatively a few individuals using the standing government as their tool; for, in the outset, the people would not have consented to this measure.

This American government,—what is it but a tradition, 2 though a recent one, endeavoring to transmit itself unimpaired to posterity, but each instant losing some of its integrity? It has not the vitality and force of a single living man; for a single man can bend it to his will. It is a sort of wooden gun to the people themselves; and, if ever they should use it in earnest as a real one against each other, it will surely split. But it is not the less necessary for this; for the people must have some complicated machinery or other, and hear its din, to satisfy that idea of government which they have. Governments show thus how successfully men can be imposed on, even impose on themselves, for their own advantage. It is excellent, we must all allow; yet this government never of itself furthered any enterprise, but by the alacrity with which it got out of its way. *It* does not keep the country free. *It* does not settle the West. *It* does not educate. The character inherent in the American people has done all that has been accomplished; and it would have done somewhat more, if the government had not sometimes got in its way. For government is an expedient by which men would fain succeed in letting one another alone; and, as has been said, when it is most expedient, the governed are most let alone by it. Trade and commerce, if they were not made of India rubber, would never manage to bounce over the obstacles which legislators are continually putting in their way; and, if one were to judge these men wholly by the effects of their actions, and not partly by their intentions, they would deserve to be classed and punished with those mischievous persons who put obstructions on the railroads.

But, to speak practically and as a citizen, unlike those who call 3 themselves no-government men, I ask for, not at once no government, but *at once* a better government. Let every man make known what kind of government would command his respect, and that will be one step toward obtaining it.

After all, the practical reason why, when the power is once in   4
the hands of the people, a majority are permitted, and for a long
period continue, to rule, is not because they are most likely to
be in the right, nor because this seems fairest to the minority, but
because they are physically the strongest. But a government in
which the majority rule in all cases cannot be based on justice,
even as far as men understand it. Can there not be a government
in which majorities do not virtually decide right and wrong, but
conscience?—in which majorities decide only those questions to
which the rule of expediency is applicable? Must the citizen ever
for a moment, or in the least degree, resign his conscience to the
legislator? Why has every man a conscience, then? I think that
we should be men first, and subjects afterward. It is not desirable
to cultivate a respect for the law, so much as for the right. The
only obligation which I have a right to assume, is to do at any
time what I think right. It is truly enough said, that a corporation
has no conscience; but a corporation of conscientious men is a
corporation *with* a conscience. Law never made men a whit more
just; and, by means of their respect for it, even the well-disposed
are daily made the agents of injustice. A common and natural
result of an undue respect for law is, that you may see a file of
soldiers, colonel, captain, corporal, privates, powder-monkeys
and all, marching in admirable order over hill and dale to the
wars, against their wills, aye, against their common sense and
consciences, which makes it very steep marching indeed, and
produces a palpitation of the heart. They have no doubt that it is
a damnable business in which they are concerned; they are all
peaceably inclined. Now, what are they? Men at all? or small
moveable forts and magazines, at the service of some
unscrupulous man in power? Visit the Navy Yard, and behold
a marine, such a man as an American government can make, or
such as it can make a man with its black arts, a mere shadow and
reminiscence of humanity, a man laid out alive and standing,
and already, as one may say, buried under arms with funeral
accompaniments, though it may be

"Not a drum was heard, not a funeral note,
As his corse to the ramparts we hurried;
Not a soldier discharged his farewell shot
O'er the grave where our hero we buried."

The mass of men serve the State thus, not as men mainly, but   5
as machines, with their bodies. They are the standing army, and

the militia, jailers, constables, *posse comitatus,* &c. In most cases there is no free exercise whatever of the judgment or of the moral sense; but they put themselves on a level with wood and earth and stones; and wooden men can perhaps be manufactured that will serve the purpose as well. Such command no more respect than men of straw, or a lump of dirt. They have the same sort of worth only as horses and dogs. Yet such as these even are commonly esteemed good citizens. Others, as most legislators, politicians, lawyers, ministers, and office-holders, serve the State chiefly with their heads; and, as they rarely make any moral distinctions, they are as likely to serve the devil, without intending it, as God. A very few, as heroes, patriots, martyrs, reformers in the great sense, and *men,* serve the State with their consciences also, and so necessarily resist it for the most part; and they are commonly treated by it as enemies. A wise man will only be useful as a man, and will not submit to be "clay," and "stop a hole to keep the wind away," but leave that office to his dust at least:—

> "I am too high-born to be propertied,
> To be a secondary at control,
> Or useful serving-man and instrument
> To any sovereign state throughout the world."

He who gives himself entirely to his fellow-men appears to   6
them useless and selfish; but he who gives himself partially to
them is pronounced a benefactor and philanthropist.

How does it become a man to behave toward this American   7
government to-day? I answer that he cannot without disgrace
be associated with it. I cannot for an instant recognize that
political organization as *my* government which is the *slave's*
government also.

All men recognize the right of revolution; that is, the right to   8
refuse allegiance to, and to resist, the government, when its
tyranny or its inefficiency are great and unendurable. But almost
all say that such is not the case now. But such was the case, they
think, in the Revolution of '75. If one were to tell me that this was
a bad government because it taxed certain foreign commodities
brought to its ports, it is most probable that I should not make
an ado about it, for I can do without them: all machines have their
friction; and possibly this does enough good to counterbalance
the evil. At any rate, it is a great evil to make a stir about it. But
when the friction comes to have its machine, and oppression and
robbery are organized, I say, let us not have such a machine any

longer. In other words, when a sixth of the population of a nation which has undertaken to be the refuge of liberty are slaves, and a whole country is unjustly overrun and conquered by a foreign army, and subjected to military law, I think that it is not too soon for honest men to rebel and revolutionize. What makes this duty the more urgent is the fact that the country so overrun is not our own, but ours is the invading army.

Paley, a common authority with many on moral questions, in   9 his chapter on the "Duty of Submission to Civil Government," resolves all civil obligation into expediency; and he proceeds to say, that "so long as the interest of the whole society requires it, that is, so long as the established government cannot be resisted or changed without public inconveniency, it is the will of God that the established government be obeyed, and no longer."— "This principle being admitted, the justice of every particular case of resistance is reduced to a computation of the quantity of the danger and grievance on the one side, and of the probability and expense of redressing it on the other." Of this, he says, every man shall judge for himself. But Paley appears never to have contemplated those cases to which the rule of expediency does not apply, in which a people, as well as an individual, must do justice, cost what it may. If I have unjustly wrested a plank from a drowning man, I must restore it to him though I drown myself. This, according to Paley, would be inconvenient. But he that would save his life, in such a case, shall lose it. This people must cease to hold slaves, and to make war on Mexico, though it cost them their existence as a people.

In their practice, nations agree with Paley; but does any   10 one think that Massachusetts does exactly what is right at the present crisis?

> "A drab of state, a cloth-o'-silver slut,
> To have her train borne up, and her soul trail in the dirt."

Practically speaking, the opponents to a reform in Massachusetts are not a hundred thousand politicians at the South, but a hundred thousand merchants and farmers here, who are more interested in commerce and agriculture than they are in humanity, and are not prepared to do justice to the slave and to Mexico, *cost what it may.* I quarrel not with far-off foes, but with those who, near at home, co-operate with, and do the bidding of those far away, and without whom the latter would be harmless. We are accustomed to say, that the mass of men are unprepared; but improvement is slow, because the few are not materially wiser or better than the many. It is not so important that many should be as good as you, as that there be some absolute goodness somewhere; for that will leaven the whole lump. There are thousands who are *in opinion* opposed to slavery and to the war, who yet in effect do nothing to put an end to them; who, esteeming themselves children of Washington and Franklin, sit down with their hands in their pockets, and say that they know not what to do, and do nothing; who even postpone the question of freedom to the question of free-trade, and quietly read the prices-current along with the latest advices from Mexico, after dinner, and, it may be, fall asleep over them both. What is the price-current of an honest man and patriot to-day? They hesitate, and they regret, and sometimes they petition; but they do nothing in earnest and with effect. They will wait, well disposed, for others to remedy the evil, that they may no longer have it to regret. At most, they give only a cheap vote, and a feeble countenance and Godspeed, to the right, as it goes by them. There are nine hundred and ninety-nine patrons of virtue to one virtuous man; but it is easier to deal with the real possessor of a thing than with the temporary guardian of it.

All voting is a sort of gaming, like chequers or backgammon, 11 with a slight moral tinge to it, a playing with right and wrong, with moral questions; and betting naturally accompanies it. The character of the voters is not staked. I cast my vote, perchance, as I think right; but I am not vitally concerned that that right should prevail. I am willing to leave it to the majority. Its obligation, therefore, never exceeds that of expediency. Even voting *for the right* is *doing* nothing for it. It is only expressing to men feebly your desire that it should prevail. A wise man will not leave the right to the mercy of chance, nor wish it to prevail through the power of the majority. There is but little virtue in the action of masses of men. When the majority shall at length vote for the abolition of slavery, it will be because they are indifferent to slavery, or because there is but little slavery left to be abolished by their vote. *They* will then be the only slaves. Only *his* vote can hasten the abolition of slavery who asserts his own freedom by his vote.

I hear of a convention to be held at Baltimore, or elsewhere, 12 for the selection of a candidate for the Presidency, made up chiefly of editors, and men who are politicians by profession; but I think, what is it to any independent, intelligent, and respectable man

what decision they may come to, shall we not have the advantage
of his wisdom and honesty, nevertheless? Can we not count upon
some independent votes? Are there not many individuals in the
country who do not attend conventions? But no: I find that the
respectable man, so called, has immediately drifted from his
position, and despairs of his country, when his country has more
reason to despair of him. He forthwith adopts one of the
candidates thus selected as the only *available* one, thus proving
that he is himself *available* for any purposes of the demagogue. His
vote is of no more worth than that of any unprincipled foreigner
or hireling native, who may have been bought. Oh for a man
who is a *man*, and, as my neighbor says, has a bone in his back
which you cannot pass your hand through! Our statistics are at
fault: the population has been returned too large. How many
men are there to a square thousand miles in this country? Hardly
one. Does not America offer any inducement for men to settle
here? The American has dwindled into an Odd Fellow,—one
who may be known by the development of his organ of
gregariousness, and a manifest lack of intellect and cheerful self-
reliance; whose first and chief concern, on coming into the world,
is to see that the almshouses are in good repair; and, before yet he
has lawfully donned the virile garb, to collect a fund for the
support of the widows and orphans that may be; who, in short,
ventures to live only by the aid of the mutual insurance company,
which has promised to bury him decently.

    It is not a man's duty, as a matter of course, to devote himself 13
to the eradication of any, even the most enormous wrong; he
may still properly have other concerns to engage him; but it is his
duty, at least, to wash his hands of it, and, if he gives it no
thought longer, not to give it practically his support. If I devote
myself to other pursuits and contemplations, I must first see, at
least, that I do not pursue them sitting upon another man's
shoulders. I must get off him first, that he may pursue his
contemplations too. See what gross inconsistency is tolerated. I
have heard some of my townsmen say, "I should like to have
them order me out to help put down an insurrection of the
slaves, or to march to Mexico,—see if I would go;" and yet these
very men have each, directly by their allegiance, and so
indirectly, at least, by their money, furnished a substitute. The
soldier is applauded who refuses to serve in an unjust war by
those who do not refuse to sustain the unjust government which
makes the war; is applauded by those whose own act and

authority he disregards and sets at nought; as if the State were penitent to that degree that it hired one to scourge it while it sinned, but not to that degree that it left off sinning for a moment. Thus, under the name of order and civil government, we are all made at last to pay homage to and support our own meanness. After the first blush of sin, comes its indifference; and from immoral it becomes, as it were, *un*moral, and not quite unnecessary to that life which we have made.

The broadest and most prevalent error requires the most 14 disinterested virtue to sustain it. The slight reproach to which the virtue of patriotism is commonly liable, the noble are most likely to incur. Those who, while they disapprove of the character and measures of a government, yield to it their allegiance and support, are undoubtedly its most conscientious supporters, and so frequently the most serious obstacles to reform. Some are petitioning the State to dissolve the Union, to disregard the requisitions of the President. Why do they not dissolve it themselves,—the union between themselves and the State,—and refuse to pay their quota into its treasury? Do not they stand in the same relation to the State, that the State does to the Union? And have not the same reasons prevented the State from resisting the Union, which have prevented them from resisting the State?

How can a man be satisfied to entertain an opinion merely, 15 and enjoy *it*? Is there any enjoyment in it, if his opinion is that he is aggrieved? If you are cheated out of a single dollar by your neighbor, you do not rest satisfied with knowing that you are cheated, or with saying that you are cheated, or even with petitioning him to pay you your due; but you take effectual steps at once to obtain the full amount, and see that you are never cheated again. Action from principle,—the perception and the performance of right,—changes things and relations; it is essentially revolutionary, and does not consist wholly with anything which was. It not only divides states and churches, it divides families; aye, it divides the *individual*, separating the diabolical in him from the divine.

Unjust laws exist; shall we be content to obey them, or shall 16 we endeavor to amend them, and obey them until we have succeeded, or shall we transgress them at once? Men generally, under such a government as this, think that they ought to wait until they have persuaded the majority to alter them. They think that, if they should resist, the remedy would be worse than the evil. But it is the fault of the government itself that the remedy *is* worse than the evil. *It* makes it worse. Why is it not more apt to anticipate and provide for reform? Why does it not cherish its wise minority? Why does it cry and resist before it is hurt? Why does it not encourage its citizens to be on the alert to point out its faults, and *do* better than it would have them? Why does it always crucify Christ, and excommunicate Copernicus and Luther, and pronounce Washington and Franklin rebels?

One would think, that a deliberate and practical denial of its   17 authority was the only offence never contemplated by government; else, why has it not assigned its definite, its suitable and proportionate penalty? If a man who has no property refuses but once to earn nine shillings for the State, he is put in prison for a period unlimited by any law that I know, and determined only by the discretion of those who placed him there; but if he should steal ninety times nine shillings from the State, he is soon permitted to go at large again.

If the injustice is part of the necessary friction of the machine   18 of government, let it go, let it go; perchance it will wear smooth,— certainly the machine will wear out. If the injustice has a spring, or a pulley, or a rope, or a crank, exclusively for itself, then perhaps you may consider whether the remedy will not be worse than the evil; but if it is of such a nature that it requires you to be the agent of injustice to another, then, I say, break the law. Let your life be a counter friction to stop the machine. What I have to do is to see, at any rate, that I do not lend myself to the wrong which I condemn.

As for adopting the ways which the State has provided for   19 remedying the evil, I know not of such ways. They take too much time, and a man's life will be gone. I have other affairs to attend to. I came into this world, not chiefly to make this a good place to live in, but to live in it, be it good or bad. A man has not every thing to do, but something; and because he cannot do *every thing*, it is not necessary that he should do *something* wrong. It is not my business to be petitioning the governor or the legislature any more than it is theirs to petition me; and, if they should not hear my petition, what should I do then? But in this case the State has provided no way: its very Constitution is the evil. This may seem to be harsh and stubborn and unconciliatory; but it is to treat with the utmost kindness and consideration the only spirit that can appreciate or deserves it. So is all change for the better, like birth and death which convulse the body.

I do not hesitate to say, that those who call themselves 20
abolitionists should at once effectually withdraw their support,
both in person and property, from the government of
Massachusetts, and not wait till they constitute a majority of one,
before they suffer the right to prevail through them. I think that
it is enough if they have God on their side, without waiting for
that other one. Moreover, any man more right than his neighbors,
constitutes a majority of one already.

I meet this American government, or its representative the 21
State government, directly, and face to face, once a year, no
more, in the person of its tax-gatherer; this is the only mode in
which a man situated as I am necessarily meets it; and it then
says distinctly, Recognize me; and the simplest, the most
effectual, and, in the present posture of affairs, the
indispensablest mode of treating with it on this head, of
expressing your little satisfaction with and love for it, is to deny
it then. My civil neighbor, the tax-gatherer, is the very man I
have to deal with,—for it is, after all, with men and not with
parchment that I quarrel,—and he has voluntarily chosen to be
an agent of the government. How shall he ever know well what
he is and does as an officer of the government, or as a man,
until he is obliged to consider whether he shall treat me, his
neighbor, for whom he has respect, as a neighbor and well-
disposed man, or as a maniac and disturber of the peace, and see
if he can get over this obstruction to his neighborliness without
a ruder and more impetuous thought or speech corresponding
with his action? I know this well, that if one thousand, if one
hundred, if ten men whom I could name,—if ten *honest* men
only,—aye, if *one* HONEST man, in this State of Massachusetts,
ceasing to hold slaves, were actually to withdraw from this
copartnership, and be locked up in the county jail therefor, it
would be the abolition of slavery in America. For it matters not
how small the beginning may seem to be: what is once well
done is done forever. But we love better to talk about it: that
we say is our mission. Reform keeps many scores of newspapers
in its service, but not one man. If my esteemed neighbor, the
State's ambassador, who will devote his days to the settlement
of the question of human rights in the Council Chamber, instead
of being threatened with the prisons of Carolina, were to sit
down the prisoner of Massachusetts, that State which is so
anxious to foist the sin of slavery upon her sister,—though at
present she can discover only an act of inhospitality to be the

ground of a quarrel with her,—the Legislature would not wholly waive the subject the following winter.

Under a government which imprisons any unjustly, the true 22 place for a just man is also a prison. The proper place to-day, the only place which Massachusetts has provided for her freer and less desponding spirits, is in her prisons, to be put out and locked out of the State by her own act, as they have already put themselves out by their principles. It is there that the fugitive slave, and the Mexican prisoner on parole, and the Indian come to plead the wrongs of his race, should find them; on that separate, but more free and honorable ground, where the State places those who are not *with* her, but *against* her,—the only house in a slave-state in which a free man can abide with honor. If any think that their influence would be lost there, and their voices no longer afflict the ear of the State, that they would not be as an enemy within its walls, they do not know by how much truth is stronger than error, nor how much more eloquently and effectively he can combat injustice who has experienced a little in his own person. Cast your whole vote, not a strip of paper merely, but your whole influence. A minority is powerless while it conforms to the majority; it is not even a minority then; but it is irresistible when it clogs by its whole weight. If the alternative is to keep all just men in prison, or give up war and slavery, the State will not hesitate which to choose. If a thousand men were not to pay their tax-bills this year, that would not be a violent and bloody measure, as it would be to pay them, and enable the State to commit violence and shed innocent blood. This is, in fact, the definition of a peaceable revolution, if any such is possible. If the tax-gatherer, or any other public officer, asks me, as one has done, "But what shall I do?" my answer is, "If you really wish to do any thing, resign your office." When the subject has refused allegiance, and the officer has resigned his office, then the revolution is accomplished. But even suppose blood should flow. Is there not a sort of blood shed when the conscience is wounded? Through this wound a man's real manhood and immortality flow out, and he bleeds to an everlasting death. I see this blood flowing now.

I have contemplated the imprisonment of the offender, rather 23 than the seizure of his goods,—though both will serve the same purpose,—because they who assert the purest right, and consequently are most dangerous to a corrupt State, commonly have not spent much time in accumulating property. To such the

State renders comparatively small service, and a slight tax is wont to appear exorbitant, particularly if they are obliged to earn it by special labor with their hands. If there were one who lived wholly without the use of money, the State itself would hesitate to demand it of him. But the rich man—not to make any invidious comparison—is always sold to the institution which makes him rich. Absolutely speaking, the more money, the less virtue; for money comes between a man and his objects, and obtains them for him; and it was certainly no great virtue to obtain it. It puts to rest many questions which he would otherwise be taxed to answer; while the only new question which it puts is the hard but superfluous one, how to spend it. Thus his moral ground is taken from under his feet. The opportunities of living are diminished in proportion as what are called the "means" are increased. The best thing a man can do for his culture when he is rich is to endeavor to carry out those schemes which he entertained when he was poor. Christ answered the Herodians according to their condition. "Show me the tribute-money," said he;—and one took a penny out of his pocket;—if you use money which has the image of Cæsar on it, and which he has made current and valuable, that is, *if you are men of the State*, and gladly enjoy the advantages of Cæsar's government, then pay him back some of his own when he demands it; "Render therefore to Cæsar that which is Cæsar's, and to God those things which are God's,"—leaving them no wiser than before as to which was which; for they did not wish to know.

When I converse with the freest of my neighbors, I perceive 24 that, whatever they may say about the magnitude and seriousness of the question, and their regard for the public tranquillity, the long and the short of the matter is, that they cannot spare the protection of the existing government, and they dread the consequences of disobedience to it to their property and families. For my own part, I should not like to think that I ever rely on the protection of the State. But, if I deny the authority of the State when it presents its tax-bill, it will soon take and waste all my property, and so harass me and my children without end. This is hard. This makes it impossible for a man to live honestly and at the same time comfortably in outward respects. It will not be worth the while to accumulate property; that would be sure to go again. You must hire or squat somewhere, and raise but a small crop, and eat that soon. You must live within yourself, and depend upon yourself, always tucked up and ready for a start, and not have many affairs. A man may grow rich in Turkey even, if he will be in all respects a good subject of the Turkish government. Confucius said,— "If a State is governed by the principles of reason, poverty and misery are subjects of shame; if a State is not governed by the principles of reason, riches and honors are the subjects of shame." No: until I want the protection of Massachusetts to be extended to me in some distant southern port, where my liberty is endangered, or until I am bent solely on building up an estate at home by peaceful enterprise, I can afford to refuse allegiance to Massachusetts, and her right to my property and life. It costs me less in every sense to incur the penalty of disobedience to the State than it would to obey. I should feel as if I were worth less in that case.

Some years ago, the State met me in behalf of the church,   25
and commanded me to pay a certain sum toward the support of a clergyman whose preaching my father attended, but never I myself. "Pay it," it said, "or be locked up in the jail." I declined to pay. But, unfortunately, another man saw fit to pay it. I did not see why the schoolmaster should be taxed to support the priest, and not the priest the schoolmaster; for I was not the State's schoolmaster, but I supported myself by voluntary subscription. I did not see why the lyceum should not present its tax-bill, and have the State to back its demand, as well as the church. However, at the request of the selectmen, I condescended to make some such statement as this in writing:—"Know all men by these presents, that I, Henry Thoreau, do not wish to be regarded as a member of any incorporated society which I have not joined." This I gave to the town clerk; and he has it. The State, having thus learned that I did not wish to be regarded as a member of that church, has never made a like demand on me since; though it said that it must adhere to its original presumption that time. If I had known how to name them, I should then have signed off in detail from all the societies which I never signed on to; but I did not know where to find a complete list.

I have paid no poll-tax for six years. I was put into a jail once   26
on this account, for one night; and, as I stood considering the walls of solid stone, two or three feet thick, the door of wood and iron, a foot thick, and the iron grating which strained the light, I could not help being struck with the foolishness of that institution which treated me as if I were mere flesh and blood and bones, to be locked up. I wondered that it should have concluded at length that this was the best use it could put me to,

and had never thought to avail itself of my services in some way. I saw that, if there was a wall of stone between me and my townsmen, there was a still more difficult one to climb or break through, before they could get to be as free as I was. I did not for a moment feel confined, and the walls seemed a great waste of stone and mortar. I felt as if I alone of all my townsmen had paid my tax. They plainly did not know how to treat me, but behaved like persons who are underbred. In every threat and in every compliment there was a blunder; for they thought that my chief desire was to stand the other side of that stone wall. I could not but smile to see how industriously they locked the door on my meditations, which followed them out again without let or hindrance, and *they* were really all that was dangerous. As they could not reach me, they had resolved to punish my body; just as boys, if they cannot come at some person against whom they have a spite, will abuse his dog. I saw that the State was half-witted, that it was timid as a lone woman with her silver spoons, and that it did not know its friends from its foes, and I lost all my remaining respect for it, and pitied it.

Thus the State never intentionally confronts a man's sense, 27 intellectual or moral, but only his body, his senses. It is not armed with superior wit or honesty, but with superior physical strength. I was not born to be forced. I will breathe after my own fashion. Let us see who is the strongest. What force has a multitude? They only can force me who obey a higher law than I. They force me to become like themselves. I do not hear of *men* being *forced* to live this way or that by masses of men. What sort of life were that to live? When I meet a government which says to me, "Your money or your life," why should I be in haste to give it my money? It may be in a great strait, and not know what to do: I cannot help that. It must help itself; do as I do. It is not worth the while to snivel about it. I am not responsible for the successful working of the machinery of society. I am not the son of the engineer. I perceive that, when an acorn and a chestnut fall side by side, the one does not remain inert to make way for the other, but both obey their own laws, and spring and grow and flourish as best they can, till one, perchance, overshadows and destroys the other. If a plant cannot live according to its nature, it dies; and so a man.

The night in prison was novel and interesting enough. The prisoners in 28 their shirt-sleeves were enjoying a chat and the evening air in the doorway, when I entered. But the jailer said, "Come, boys, it is time to lock up;" and so they dispersed, and I heard the sound of their steps returning into the hollow apartments. My room-mate was introduced to me by the jailer, as "a first-rate fellow and a clever man." When the door was locked, he showed me where to hang my hat, and how he managed matters there. The rooms were whitewashed once a month; and this one, at least, was the whitest, most simply furnished, and probably the neatest apartment in the town. He naturally wanted to know where I came from, and what brought me there; and, when I had told him, I asked him in my turn how he came there, presuming him to be an honest man, of course; and, as the world goes, I believe he was. "Why," said he, "they accuse me of burning a barn; but I never did it." As near as I could discover, he had probably gone to bed in a barn when drunk, and smoked his pipe there; and so a barn was burnt. He had the reputation of being a clever man, had been there some three months waiting for his trial to come on, and would have to wait as much longer; but he was quite domesticated and contented, since he got his board for nothing, and thought that he was well treated.

He occupied one window, and I the other; and I saw, that, if one 29 stayed there long, his principal business would be to look out the window. I had soon read all the tracts that were left there, and examined where former prisoners had broken out, and where a grate had been sawed off, and heard the history of the various occupants of that room; for I found that even here there was a history and a gossip which never circulated beyond the walls of the jail. Probably this is the only house in the town where verses are composed, which are afterward printed in a circular form, but not published. I was shown quite a long list of verses which were composed by some young men who had been detected in an attempt to escape, who avenged themselves by singing them.

I pumped my fellow-prisoner as dry as I could, for fear I should 30 never see him again; but at length he showed me which was my bed, and left me to blow out the lamp.

It was like travelling into a far country, such as I had never expected 31 to behold, to lie there for one night. It seemed to me that I never had heard the town-clock strike before, nor the evening sounds of the village; for we slept with the windows open, which were inside the grating. It was to see my native village in the light of the Middle Ages, and our Concord was turned into a Rhine stream, and visions of knights and castles passed before me. They were the voices of old burghers that I heard in the streets. I was an involuntary spectator and auditor of whatever was done and said in the kitchen of the adjacent village-inn,— a wholly new and rare experience to me. It was a closer view of my native town. I was fairly inside of it. I never had seen its institutions before. This is one of its peculiar institutions; for it is a shire town. I began to comprehend what its inhabitants were about.

In the morning, our breakfasts were put through the hole in the   32
door, in small oblong-square tin pans, made to fit, and holding a pint of
chocolate, with brown bread, and an iron spoon. When they called for the
vessels again, I was green enough to return what bread I had left; but
my comrade seized it, and said that I should lay that up for lunch or
dinner. Soon after, he was let out to work at haying in a neighboring
field, whither he went every day, and would not be back till noon; so he
bade me good-day, saying that he doubted if he should see me again.

When I came out of prison,—for some one interfered, and paid the   33
tax,—I did not perceive that great changes had taken place on the
common, such as he observed who went in a youth and emerged a
tottering and gray-headed man; and yet a change had to my eyes come
over the scene,—the town, and State, and country,—greater than any
that mere time could effect. I saw yet more distinctly the State in which
I lived. I saw to what extent the people among whom I lived could be
trusted as good neighbors and friends; that their friendship was for
summer weather only; that they did not greatly propose to do right;
that they were a distinct race from me by their prejudices and
superstitions, as the Chinamen and Malays are; that, in their sacrifices to
humanity, they ran no risks, not even to their property; that, after all,
they were not so noble but they treated the thief as he had treated them,
and hoped, by a certain outward observance and a few prayers, and by
walking in a particular straight though useless path from time to time,
to save their souls. This may be to judge my neighbors harshly; for I
believe that many of them are not aware that they have such an
institution as the jail in their village.

It was formerly the custom in our village, when a poor debtor came   34
out of jail, for his acquaintances to salute him, looking through their
fingers, which were crossed to represent the grating of a jail window,
"How do ye do?" My neighbors did not thus salute me, but first looked
at me, and then at one another, as if I had returned from a long journey.
I was put into jail as I was going to the shoemaker's to get a shoe which
was mended. When I was let out the next morning, I proceeded to finish
my errand, and, having put on my mended shoe, joined a huckleberry
party, who were impatient to put themselves under my conduct; and in
half an hour,—for the horse was soon tackled,—was in the midst of a
huckleberry field, on one of our highest hills, two miles off; and then the
State was nowhere to be seen.

This is the whole history of "My Prisons."   35

I have never declined paying the highway tax, because I am   36
as desirous of being a good neighbor as I am of being a bad
subject; and, as for supporting schools, I am doing my part to
educate my fellow-countrymen now. It is for no particular item
in the tax-bill that I refuse to pay it. I simply wish to refuse

allegiance to the State, to withdraw and stand aloof from it effectually. I do not care to trace the course of my dollar, if I could, till it buys a man, or a musket to shoot one with,—the dollar is innocent,—but I am concerned to trace the effects of my allegiance. In fact, I quietly declare war with the State, after my fashion, though I will still make what use and get what advantage of her I can, as is usual in such cases.

If others pay the tax which is demanded of me, from a 37 sympathy with the State, they do but what they have already done in their own case, or rather they abet injustice to a greater extent than the State requires. If they pay the tax from a mistaken interest in the individual taxed, to save his property, or prevent his going to jail, it is because they have not considered wisely how far they let their private feelings interfere with the public good.

This, then, is my position at present. But one cannot be too 38 much on his guard in such a case, lest his action be biased by obstinacy, or an undue regard for the opinions of men. Let him see that he does only what belongs to himself and to the hour.

I think sometimes, Why, this people mean well; they are only 39 ignorant; they would do better if they knew how: why give your neighbors this pain to treat you as they are not inclined to? But I think, again, this is no reason why I should do as they do, or permit others to suffer much greater pain of a different kind. Again, I sometimes say to myself, When many millions of men, without heat, without ill-will, without personal feeling of any kind, demand of you a few shillings only, without the possibility, such is their constitution, of retracting or altering their present demand, and without the possibility, on your side, of appeal to any other millions, why expose yourself to this overwhelming brute force? You do not resist cold and hunger, the winds and the waves, thus obstinately; you quietly submit to a thousand similar necessities. You do not put your head into the fire. But just in proportion as I regard this as not wholly a brute force, but partly a human force, and consider that I have relations to those millions as to so many millions of men, and not of mere brute or inanimate things, I see that appeal is possible, first and instantaneously, from them to the Maker of them, and, secondly, from them to themselves. But, if I put my head deliberately into the fire, there is no appeal to fire or to the Maker of fire, and I have only myself to blame. If I could convince myself that I have any right to be satisfied with men as they are, and to treat them accordingly, and not according, in some respects, to my requisitions and expectations of what they and I ought to be, then, like a good Mussulman and fatalist, I should endeavor to be satisfied with things as they are, and say it is the will of God. And, above all, there is this difference between resisting this and a purely brute or natural force, that I can resist this with some effect; but I cannot expect, like Orpheus, to change the nature of the rocks and trees and beasts.

I do not wish to quarrel with any man or nation. I do not 40 wish to split hairs, to make fine distinctions, or set myself up as better than my neighbors. I seek rather, I may say, even an excuse for conforming to the laws of the land. I am but too ready to conform to them. Indeed I have reason to suspect myself on this head; and each year, as the tax-gatherer comes round, I find myself disposed to review the acts and position of the general and state governments, and the spirit of the people, to discover a pretext for conformity. I believe that the State will soon be able to take all my work of this sort out of my hands, and then I shall be no better a patriot than my fellow-countrymen. Seen from a lower point of view, the Constitution, with all its faults, is very good; the law and the courts are very respectable; even this State and this American government are, in many respects, very admirable and rare things, to be thankful for, such as a great many have described them; but seen from a point of view a little higher, they are what I have described them; seen from a higher still, and the highest, who shall say what they are, or that they are worth looking at or thinking of at all?

However, the government does not concern me much, and I 41 shall bestow the fewest possible thoughts on it. It is not many moments that I live under a government, even in this world. If a man is thought-free, fancy-free, imagination-free, that which *is not* never for a long time appearing *to be* to him, unwise rulers or reformers cannot fatally interrupt him.

I know that most men think differently from myself; but 42 those whose lives are by profession devoted to the study of these or kindred subjects, content me as little as any. Statesmen and legislators, standing so completely within the institution, never distinctly and nakedly behold it. They speak of moving society, but have no resting-place without it. They may be men of a certain experience and discrimination, and have no doubt invented ingenious and even useful systems, for which we sincerely thank them; but all their wit and usefulness lie within certain not very wide limits. They are wont to forget that the world is not governed by policy and expediency. Webster never goes behind government, and so cannot speak with authority about it. His words are wisdom to those legislators who contemplate no essential reform in the existing government; but for thinkers, and those who legislate for all time, he never once glances at the subject. I know of those whose serene and wise speculations on this theme would soon reveal the limits of his mind's range and hospitality. Yet, compared with the cheap professions of most reformers, and the still cheaper wisdom and eloquence of politicians in general, his are almost the only sensible and valuable words, and we thank Heaven for him. Comparatively, he is always strong, original, and, above all, practical. Still his quality is not wisdom, but prudence. The lawyer's truth is not Truth, but consistency or a consistent expediency. Truth is always in harmony with herself, and is not concerned chiefly to reveal the justice that may consist with wrong-doing. He well deserves to be called, as he has been called, the Defender of the Constitution. There are really no blows to be given by him but defensive ones. He is not a leader, but a follower. His leaders are the men of '87. "I have never made an effort," he says, "and never propose to make an effort; I have never countenanced an effort, and never mean to countenance an effort, to disturb the arrangement as originally made, by which the various States came into the Union." Still thinking of the sanction which the Constitution gives to slavery, he says, "Because it was a part of the original compact,—let it stand." Notwithstanding his special acuteness and ability, he is unable to take a fact out of its merely political relations, and behold it as it lies absolutely to be disposed of by the intellect,—what, for instance, it behoves a man to do here in America to-day with regard to slavery, but ventures, or is driven, to make some such desperate answer as the following, while professing to speak absolutely, and as a private man,—from which what new and singular code of social duties might be inferred?—"The manner," says he, "in which the governments of those States where slavery exists are to regulate it, is for their own consideration, under their responsibility to their constituents, to the general laws of propriety, humanity, and justice, and to God. Associations formed elsewhere, springing from a feeling of humanity, or any other cause, have nothing whatever to do with it. They have never received any encouragement from me, and they never will."*

They who know of no purer sources of truth, who have traced 43 up its stream no higher, stand, and wisely stand, by the Bible and the Constitution, and drink at it there with reverence and humility; but they who behold where it comes trickling into this lake or that pool, gird up their loins once more, and continue their pilgrimage toward its fountain-head.

No man with a genius for legislation has appeared in 44 America. They are rare in the history of the world. There are orators, politicians, and eloquent men, by the thousand; but the speaker has not yet opened his mouth to speak, who is capable of settling the much-vexed questions of the day. We love eloquence for its own sake, and not for any truth which it may utter, or any heroism it may inspire. Our legislators have not yet learned the comparative value of free-trade and of freedom, of union, and of rectitude, to a nation. They have no genius or talent for comparatively humble questions of taxation and finance, commerce and manufacturers and agriculture. If we were left solely to the wordy wit of legislators in Congress for our guidance, uncorrected by the seasonable experience and the effectual complaints of the people, America would not long retain her rank among the nations. For eighteen hundred years, though perchance I have no right to say it, the New Testament has been written; yet where is the legislator who has wisdom and practical talent enough to avail himself of the light which it sheds on the science of legislation?

The authority of government, even such as I am willing to 45 submit to,—for I will cheerfully obey those who know and can do better than I, and in many things even those who neither know nor can do so well,—is still an impure one: to be strictly just, it must have the sanction and consent of the governed. It can have no pure right over my person and property but what I concede to it. The progress from an absolute to a limited monarchy, from a limited monarchy to a democracy, is a progress toward a true respect for the individual. Is a democracy, such as we know it, the last improvement possible in government? Is it not possible to take a step further towards recognizing and

*These extracts have been inserted since the Lecture was read.

organizing the rights of man? There will never be a really free and enlightened State until the State comes to recognize the individual as a higher and independent power, from which all its own power and authority are derived, and treats him accordingly. I please myself with imagining a State at last which can afford to be just to all men, and to treat the individual with respect as a neighbor; which even would not think it inconsistent with its own repose, if a few were to live aloof from it, not meddling with it, nor embraced by it, who fulfilled all the duties of neighbors and fellow-men. A State which bore this kind of fruit, and suffered it to drop off as fast as it ripened, would prepare the way for a still more perfect and glorious State, which also I have imagined, but not yet anywhere seen.

James Thurber

■ ■ ■

University Days

James Thurber (1894–1961), journalist, artist, humourist, was born in Columbus, Ohio, and attended Ohio State University, which he left in 1918. After spending time in Paris as an employee of the State Department and as a journalist, Thurber returned to the U.S. and began submitting pieces to *The New Yorker*. A brief meeting with E. B. White led in 1927 to Thurber's introduction to, and hiring a month later by, the editor of *The New Yorker*, Harold Ross, who thought that Thurber and White were old friends. Though the two barely knew each other, they did in fact become good friends, sharing an office, collaborating on a book (the humorous *Is Sex Necessary?* 1929), and enjoying a lifelong association. Thurber counted White as one of the main influences on his writing, and indeed, they both excelled at understated humour and at creating apparently effortless yet finely honed and rhythmical sentences. At *The New Yorker*, Thurber was responsible for the *Talk of the Town* department from 1927 to 1935; around the same time, he became increasingly well-known and respected for his cartoons for the magazine, which were published in several collections, including *The Seal in the Bedroom* (1932) and *Men, Women, and Dogs* (1943). Thurber is just as famous, however, for his short stories, essays, sketches, and fables, many of which he illustrated himself. Thurber's most famous short story is probably "The Secret Life of Walter Mitty," from *My World and Welcome to It*, a collection of essays and sketches published in 1942. One of Thurber's funniest and best books is the pseudo-autobiography, *My Life and Hard Times* (1933), from which the following selection comes.

I passed all the other courses that I took at my University, but I could never pass botany. This was because all botany students had to spend several hours a week in a laboratory looking through a microscope at plant cells, and I could never see through a microscope. I never once saw a cell through a microscope. This used to enrage my instructor. He would wander around the laboratory pleased with the progress all the students were making in drawing the involved and, so I am told, interesting structure of flower cells, until he came to me. I would just be standing there. 1

"I can't see anything," I would say. He would begin patiently enough, explaining how anybody can see through a microscope, but he would always end up in a fury, claiming that I could *too* see through a microscope but just pretended that I couldn't. "It takes away from the beauty of flowers anyway," I used to tell him. "We are not concerned with beauty in this course," he would say. "We are concerned solely with what I may call the mechanics of flars." "Well," I'd say. "I can't see anything." "Try it just once again," he'd say, and I would put my eye to the microscope and see nothing at all, except now and again a nebulous milky substance—a phenomenon of maladjustment. You were supposed to see a vivid, restless clockwork of sharply defined plant cells. "I see what looks like a lot of milk," I would tell him. This, he claimed, was the result of my not having adjusted the microscope properly, so he would readjust it for me, or rather, for himself. And I would look again and see milk.

I finally took a deferred pass, as they called it, and waited a 2 year and tried again. (You had to pass one of the biological sciences or you couldn't graduate.) The professor had come back from vacation brown as a berry, bright-eyed, and eager to explain cell-structure again to his classes. "Well," he said to me, cheerily, when we met in the first laboratory hour of the semester, "we're going to see cells this time, aren't we?" "Yes, sir," I said. Students to the right of me and left of me and in front of me were seeing cells; what's more, they were quietly drawing pictures of them in their notebooks. Of course, I didn't see anything.

"We'll try it," the professor said to me, grimly, "with every 3 adjustment of the microscope known to man. As God is my witness, I'll arrange this glass so that you can see cells through it or I'll give up teaching. In twenty-two years of botany, I—" He cut off abruptly for he was beginning to quiver all over, like Lionel Barrymore, and he genuinely wished to hold onto his temper; his scenes with me had taken a great deal out of him.

So we tried it with every adjustment of the microscope known 4 to man. With only one of them did I see anything but blackness or the familiar lacteal opacity, and that time I saw, to my pleasure and amazement, a variegated constellation of flecks, specks, and dots. These I hastily drew. The instructor, noting my activity, came from an adjoining desk, a smile on his lips and his eyebrows high in hope. He looked at my cell drawing. "What's that?" he demanded, with a hint of squeal in his voice. "That's what I saw," I said. "You didn't, you didn't, you *did*n't!" he screamed, losing control of his temper instantly, and he bent over and squinted into the microscope. His head snapped up. "That's your eye!" he shouted. "You've fixed the lens so that it reflects! You've drawn your eye!"

Another course that I didn't like, but somehow managed to pass, was economics. I went to that class straight from the botany class, which didn't help me any in understanding either subject. I used to get them mixed up. But not as mixed up as another student in my economics class who came there direct from a physics laboratory. He was a tackle on the football team, named Bolenciecwcz. At that time Ohio State University had one of the best football teams in the country, and Bolenciecwcz was one of its outstanding stars. In order to be eligible to play it was necessary for him to keep up in his studies, a very difficult matter, for while he was not dumber than an ox he was not any smarter. Most of his professors were lenient and helped him along. None gave him more hints, in answering questions, or asked him simpler ones than the economics professor, a thin, timid man named Bassum. One day when we were on the subject of transportation and distribution, it came Bolenciecwcz's turn to answer a question. "Name one means of transportation," the professor said to him. No light came into the big tackle's eyes. "Just any means of transportation," said the professor. Bolenciecwcz sat staring at him. "That is," pursued the professor, "any medium, agency, or method of going from one place to another." Bolenciecwcz had the look of a man who is being led into a trap. "You may choose among steam, horse-drawn, or electrically propelled vehicles," said the instructor. "I might suggest the one which we commonly take in making long journeys across land." There was a profound silence in which everybody stirred uneasily, including Bolenciecwcz and Mr. Bassum. Mr. Bassum abruptly broke this silence in an amazing manner. "Choo-choo-choo," he said, in a low voice, and turned instantly scarlet. He glanced appealingly around the room. All of us, of course, shared Mr. Bassum's desire that Bolenciecwcz should stay abreast of the class in economics, for the Illinois game, one of the hardest and most important of the season, was only a week off. "Toot, toot, too-toooooooot!" some student with a deep voice moaned, and we all looked encouragingly at Bolenciecwcz. Somebody else gave a fine imitation of a locomotive letting off steam. Mr. Bassum himself rounded off the little show. "Ding, dong, ding, dong," he said, hopefully. Bolenciecwcz was staring

5

at the floor now, trying to think, his great brow furrowed, his huge hands rubbing together, his face red.

"How did you come to college this year, Mr. Bolenciecwcz?" 6 asked the professor. "*Chuf*fa chuffa, *chuf*fa chuffa."

"M'father sent me," said the football player.   7

"What on?" asked Bassum.   8

"I git an 'lowance," said the tackle, in a low, husky voice, 9 obviously embarrassed.

"No, no," said Bassum. "Name a means of transportation. 10 What did you *ride* here on?"

"Train," said Bolenciecwcz.   11

"Quite right," said the professor. "Now, Mr. Nugent, will 12 you tell us—"

If I went through anguish in botany and economics—for 13 different reasons—gymnasium work was even worse. I don't even like to think about it. They wouldn't let you play games or join in the exercises with your glasses on and I couldn't see with mine off. I bumped into professors, horizontal bars, agricultural students, and swinging iron rings. Not being able to see, I could take it but I couldn't dish it out. Also, in order to pass gymnasium (and you had to pass it to graduate) you had to learn to swim if you didn't know how. I didn't like the swimming pool, I didn't like swimming, and I didn't like the swimming instructor, and after all these years I still don't. I never swam but I passed my gym work anyway, by having another student give my gymnasium number (978) and swim across the pool in my place. He was a quiet, amiable blonde youth, number 473, and he would have seen through a microscope for me if we could have got away with it, but we couldn't get away with it. Another thing I didn't like about gymnasium work was that they made you strip the day you registered. It is impossible for me to be happy when I am stripped and being asked a lot of questions. Still, I did better than a lanky agricultural student who was cross-examined just before I was. They asked each student what college he was in— that is, whether Arts, Engineering, Commerce, or Agriculture. "What college are you in?" the instructor snapped at the youth in front of me. "Ohio State University," he said promptly.

It wasn't that agricultural student but it was another a whole 14 lot like him who decided to take up journalism, possibly on the ground that when farming went to hell he could fall back on newspaper work. He didn't realize, of course, that that would be very much like falling back full-length on a kit of carpenter's tools. Haskins didn't seem cut out for journalism, being too embarrassed to talk to anybody and unable to use a typewriter, but the editor of the college paper assigned him to the cow barns, the sheep house, the horse pavilion, and the animal husbandry department generally. This was a genuinely big "beat," for it took up five times as much ground and got ten times as great a legislative appropriation as the College of Liberal Arts. The agricultural student knew animals, but nevertheless his stories were dull and colorlessly written. He took all afternoon on each one of them, on account of having to hunt for each letter on the typewriter. Once in a while he had to ask somebody to help him hunt. "C" and "L," in particular, were hard letters for him to find. His editor finally got pretty much annoyed at the farmer-journalist because his pieces were so uninteresting. "See here, Haskins," he snapped at him one day, "why is it we never have anything hot from you on the horse pavilion? Here we have two hundred head of horses on this campus—more than any other university in the Western Conference except Purdue—and yet you never get any real lowdown on them. Now shoot over to the horse barns and dig up something lively." Haskins shambled out and came back in about an hour; he said he had something. "Well, start it off snappily," said the editor. "Something people will read." Haskins set to work and in a couple of hours brought a sheet of typewritten paper to the desk; it was a two-hundred word story about some disease that had broken out among the horses. Its opening sentence was simple but arresting. It read: "Who has noticed the sores on the tops of the horses in the animal husbandry building?"

Ohio State was a land grant university and therefore two years of military drill was compulsory. We drilled with old Springfield rifles and studied the tactics of the Civil War even though the World War was going on at the time. At 11 o'clock each morning thousands of freshmen and sophomores used to deploy over the campus, moodily creeping up on the old chemistry building. It was good training for the kind of warfare that was waged at Shiloh but it had no connection with what was going on in Europe. Some people used to think there was German money behind it, but they didn't dare say so or they would have been thrown in jail as German spies. It was a period of muddy thought and marked, I believe, the decline of higher education in the Middle West.

As a soldier I was never any good at all. Most of the cadets 16
were glumly indifferent soldiers, but I was no good at all. Once
General Littlefield, who was commandant of the cadet corps,
popped up in front of me during regimental drill and snapped,
"You are the main trouble with this university!" I think he meant
that my type was the main trouble with the university but he
may have meant me individually. I was mediocre at drill,
certainly—that is, until my senior year. By that time I had drilled
longer than anybody else in the Western Conference, having
failed at military at the end of each preceding year so that I had
to do it all over again. I was the only senior still in uniform. The
uniform which, when new, had made me look like an interurban
railway conductor, now that it had become faded and too tight
made me look like Bert Williams in his bellboy act. This had a
definitely bad effect on my morale. Even so, I had become by
sheer practice little short of wonderful at squad manoeuvres.

One day General Littlefield picked our company out of the 17
whole regiment and tried to get it mixed up by putting it
through one movement after another as fast as we could execute
them: squads right, squads left, squads on right into line, squads
right about, squads left front into line, etc. In about three
minutes one hundred and nine men were marching in one
direction and I was marching away from them at an angle of
forty degrees, all alone. "Company, halt!" shouted General
Littlefield, "That man is the only man who has it right!" I was
made a corporal for my achievement.

The next day General Littlefield summoned me to his office. 18
He was swatting flies when I went in. I was silent and he was
silent too, for a long time. I don't think he remembered me or
why he had sent for me, but he didn't want to admit it. He
swatted some more flies, keeping his eyes on them narrowly
before he let go with the swatter. "Button up your coat!" he
snapped. Looking back on it now I can see that he meant me
although he was looking at a fly, but I just stood there. Another
fly came to rest on a paper in front of the general and began
rubbing its hind legs together. The general lifted the swatter
cautiously. I moved restlessly and the fly flew away. "You startled
him!" barked General Littlefield, looking at me severely. I said I
was sorry. "That won't help the situation!" snapped the General,
with cold military logic. I didn't see what I could do except offer
to chase some more flies toward his desk, but I didn't say
anything. He stared out the window at the faraway figures of

co-eds crossing the campus toward the library. Finally, he told me I could go. So I went. He either didn't know which cadet I was or else he forgot what he wanted to see me about. It may have been that he wished to apologize for having called me the main trouble with the university; or maybe he had decided to compliment me on my brilliant drilling of the day before and then at the last minute decided not to. I don't know. I don't think about it much any more.

Margaret Visser

■ ■ ■

Feeding, Feasts, and Females

Margaret Visser (b. 1940), academic, essayist, writer, and radio/TV personality, was born in South Africa, studied at the Sorbonne, and earned a
PhD in Classics (1980) from the University of Toronto. A self-described
"anthropologist of everyday life," Visser has explored her interest in modern and ancient myth, history, culture, food, and the arts through numerous articles and four best-selling books. Her first book, *Much Depends on
Dinner: The Extraordinary History and Mythology, Allure and Obsessions, Perils
and Taboos of an Ordinary Meal* (1986), exploring the historical, mythical,
and cultural aspects of an ordinary meal, won Britain's Glenfiddich Prize
for Food Book of the Year, and was named one of the best books of the
year by *Publishers Weekly* and the *New York Times Book Review*. In *The Rituals
of Dinner: The Origin, Evolution, Eccentricities, and Meaning of Table Manners*
(1991), Visser examined the history and culture of table manners; it was
named a *New York Times* Notable Book of the Year and received the
International Association of Culinary Professionals Literary Food Writing
Award and the Jane Grigson Prize. Visser's third book, *The Way We Are*
(1994), is a collection of short, witty essays looking at how we live, culled
from the eponymously named column Visser began writing in 1988 for
Saturday Night magazine. Her latest book, *The Geometry of Love: Space, Time,
Mystery and Meaning in an Ordinary Church* (2000), investigates the history,
folklore, theology, and architecture of the Basilica of St. Agnes, a church just
outside the walls of Rome. "Feeding, Feasts, and Females" comes from
Chapter 4 of *The Rituals of Dinner*.

■ _____ ■

Because male and female sex roles are on a purely physical level   1
complementary, gender has always been a primary metaphor
for the allocation of roles in society. The image has allowed people
to conceptualize such ideas as "Give and take," "Do what you
can, and what you are most capable of doing," "Entrust yourself
to other people when it becomes right to do so," and even "Take
their wishes into account." The sexual model can be made to say
other things also: "Protecting somebody proves the protector's
superiority," "Might must prevail," or "Some are born to privilege and others to serve the lusts of the former." Poetic connec-

tions arise, as one would expect, from a metaphor: for example, production and reproduction may find themselves linked in thought, so that sexual behaviour is felt to influence the fruits of the harvest; if sexual behaviour is unsatisfactory, there will be nothing to eat. Men may decide that they too produce "babies," in the form of food; but men are needed for women to produce human babies, therefore women must help in the fields. The actual process of eating, which begins always with mother feeding and child being fed, is also "like sex," and the perceived similarity can influence such important social decisions as where and with whom people can be permitted to live. The provision of food and the serving of dinner are often organized on a sexual model, too. Men go, get food, and give it to their wives, while women stay, receive it, cook it, and serve it forth.

In order that all these perceptions and conventional 2 distributions of power, and many others like them, might fit and operate without hitch, enormous care is taken to ensure that the sexual model translates smoothly into the social structure. Men and women differ sexually; everything must be done then to differentiate them (along the lines already perceived, of course) through the allocation and refusal of power and prestige, in kinds of employment, in clothing and socially approved physique, in carefully instilled outlook and expectation. Men and women must do different things, and doing different things will work better if they feel different things as well. If males and females are not constantly distinguished and kept separate, important features of the social structure, clear and comfortable features, might become blurred and shaky.

It has for most of history been common for men and women 3 to eat apart, especially in public. Often taboos ensure that they eat different foods, women typically being forbidden various edible substances judged dangerous either to their morality or to their reproductive powers. Eating together in private often both entails and "means" marriage: it involves sharing the same house. Ceasing to eat together is tantamount to divorce—or ceasing to "sleep together," as we still put it. Our euphemism is not merely coy; it contains the suggestion of sharing the same private space. Cooking, like digesting, is a common metaphor for pregnancy. The woman offers cooking in exchange for sex; the man offers sex in exchange for cooking. It follows that women "receive" sex as men "are fed" food. Eating can be spoken of as synonymous with the sex act itself. In the languages of the Ghanaian LoDagaa and Gonja, the verb "to eat" is frequently used for sex, covering a semantic field very similar to that of the English word "enjoy."

The conjunction of the opposite poles of femaleness and 4 maleness in the married couple is very commonly made to stand for socially and culturally vital oppositions, including one or more of the following: private and public, inside and outside, domesticity and "work," down and up, left and right, dark and light, cold and hot, back and front, curved and straight, soft and hard, still (female) and moving (male), and so forth. Being made to "stand for" these in turn enforces conformity with the expectations. If "a woman's place is in the home," her place implies all the "female" characteristics: inferiority, quietness, a longing to nurture, unwillingness to stand forth, and renunciation of the "male" claims to authority, publicity, loudness, brightness, sharpness. These qualities have a multitude of practical applications; for example, they either make a woman altogether unfit and unwilling to attend feasts, or they influence the way she behaves while participating in them.

An ancient Greek wife would not have been seen dead at 5 a symposium. She was thought—and considered herself to be— the embodiment of purity in the family. Her honour was, and had at all costs to remain, unassailable: the legitimacy of her offspring, and the honour of her menfolk, depended upon it. It was all right for *hetairai* (courtesans) to mix with revelling and orgiastic males; they were shameless women, outrageous in their freedom and lack of *tenue*. A dining room was called an *andron*, "a room for men": a woman eating there was a woman out of place, marginalized and unworthy of respect. Unphilosophically minded ancient Greeks apparently thought, as many people nowadays still do, that important ideas should never be discussed at table. Plutarch has one such symposiast put it like this: "Philosophy should no more have a part in conversation over wine than should the matron of the house." According to this view, the Persians got it right when they drank and danced with their mistresses, but never with their wives. Wives were serious, but *hetairai* and mistresses could be taken lightly. When men, therefore, were asked to a party, they left their wives at home. But a wedding feast was a crowded affair, Plutarch makes his sympotic conversationalists say elsewhere, because women were responsible for a lot of the activities at a wedding—and an invited woman must invariably come accompanied by her husband.

Formality at public events is almost invariably a male affair, 6 because it involves social rank (which has often been denied to all but the very top women) and publicity. Formality has always been contrasted with relaxation and intimacy, which are enjoyed at home, where the women have their place. (Men inhabit both spheres, public and private, whereas women have rarely done so; this one-sided overlap is one of the important inconsistencies in the scheme.) It follows that at a banquet in many traditional societies, men observe rank and precedence at table, while women serve the diners, or sit and eat in a separate place where far less ceremony is observed; they might sit in a crowd in the middle of the room, for example, while the men are ranged in order round the walls. At a Winnebago Indian feast, the men sat observing strict precedence round the periphery of the meeting house, with plenty of room between them; the women and children crowded together in a tiny space behind a screen at the back. The women have generally cooked such feasts, though occasionally men will have insisted on handling the meat (a prestigious, "masculine" food) themselves. The women may even think of being permitted to serve the food as a tremendous, and jealously guarded, privilege. Women, say the Javanese who practise the slametan feast, are *mburi*, "behind" (that is, in the kitchen; during the feast they peep through the bamboo partitions at the men as they eat), whereas men are *ngarepan*, "in front," consuming the food prepared by the women.

In nineteenth-century Japan, women were seldom invited to dinner, but if they were they were expected to sit apart, in one 7 corner of the room. In China, they feasted separately from the men, as women do in societies where there is a very strong division between the sexes. In the Ming period, the imperial women, dowagers, wives, daughters, and sisters of their men would host the wives of ministers and officials in the Inner Quarters of the Palace of Female Tranquillity. Their banquets were accompanied by female musicians. Hostesses were required, however, to offer fewer courses at dinner than the men, and to offer wine less often. It is assumed that in private, on ordinary occasions, male and female members of the imperial family ate together, as the commoners did. In the United Arab Emirates today, as in other Arab countries, women often meet and dine together, with complex and sophisticated civility.

It is with a great sense of superiority that a male host may 8
"feed" his guests but not himself partake of the meal; and a
woman who cooks and serves a dinner without eating much of it
herself may do so with a real sense of the power conferred by
the bestowal of food. (Guests always feel uncomfortable eating in
front of an abstemious host.) But it is necessary for the giver to be
present during the meal to enjoy this particular kind of ego
enhancement, for prestige is personal: it is non-existent where
there is no knowledge of the person being honoured. As late as
the nineteenth century in French peasant households, the women
would serve the men at table, but themselves eat standing, or
draw up stools by the fire and hold their dishes on their laps;
the old and the children might be expected to join them there. It
is possible, but unlikely, that such an arrangement expressed
appreciation and respect for women.

Young boys in strictly sex-segregated societies must one day 9
make the transition from living as children with the women to
joining the men. The initiation, whether accompanied or not by
ceremonial rites, is effected in large part by the young male taking
his predestined place in public life, among the men at dinner.
Girls do not take this step; they remain, in this sense, children. (To
"stay where you are," even metaphorically, is of course to cleave
to the principle of stillness and centrality which has hitherto been
so important in the symbolism of being female.) A man often
prefers a woman to keep the status of dependent child: he may
reward her for accepting this position by finding her sexually
attractive if she does so.

A woman maintains her role as mother by feeding her 10
family; some African societies are said to think of the wife as
"mother of her husband" for this reason. Food is a female
concern, and often one of the main sources of a woman's power
in the household. Women gather food, shop, choose what is to
be eaten, and cook it. Social anthropologists have long called
women the "gatekeepers" of food supplies in the house.
However, since they choose food which they know their
husbands and children like and demand, the "gatekeeper" role
is often merely executive. Women are reported to make their
cooking expressive of their feelings: they "reward" men by
producing a special dish, with particular care; they show
disapproval by not having dinner ready on time, or by refusing
to put effort into the meal. Gertrude Stein tells the story of her
French cook Hélène, who disapproved of Matisse because a

Frenchman "should not stay unexpectedly to a meal particularly if he asked the servant beforehand what there was for dinner." One could expect such behaviour from foreigners, but in a Frenchman it was unacceptable. When Matisse was invited to dinner she would, for example, serve him fried eggs, never an omelette. "It takes the same number of eggs," she coldly asserted, "and the same amount of butter, but it shows less respect." Monsieur Matisse would understand.

If an African wife refuses to cook at all, her husband cannot   11 make her do it; men are often not only incapable of cooking but forbidden to cook. In some Nigerian tribes they are not allowed even to discuss food or express directly a desire to eat: a Jukun male will say, "I am going to eat," when he means he is thirsty, and use a phrase like "I shall go into my hut" (the *kunguni*, where Jukun males eat alone) for "I want some dinner." Eating, for him, requires the kind of euphemism which in our society is reserved for sex or excretion. This attitude towards eating is part of the allocation of roles, and again it goes back to the sexual model: "giving food" for women corresponds to "giving sex" for men; it would be extremely confusing to do things the other way round. It is fairly common for a man to refuse to eat what his wife has cooked, as a sign of his displeasure; he is protected, of course, from having to do without food altogether if he has several wives. A further connection between food and sex is suggested by the fact that a polygamous male usually eats food prepared by the wife he is currently sleeping with.

Brewing beer is an ancient female preserve; and where beer   12 is central to the economy and nutrition of a society—as it often still is in Africa, among South American Indians, and elsewhere— control over it naturally becomes a source of female power. It may link up with another commonly traditional female skill and responsibility: that of making and controlling the use of clay pots. (The ancient Greek god Dionysus—feminine in so much of his nature—had power both over wine and over the area of Athens called Ceramicus, where pots were made.) We have seen how the Newar women of Nepal must personally serve the beer they have made, even at a public feast. Among the LoDagaa of Ghana, a woman's good beer can turn her home into a beer house, a place where people gather to exchange news and gossip. She sells her product, and pours it out for her clients, always setting aside a calabash of it for herself to show she has not poisoned the batch. She plays a role rather like that of European society hostesses who used to keep "open house" or a "salon" on certain days of the week where people could collect together and socialize. The hostess of a tea party, like the LoDagaa breweress, must pour the tea.

Because food and drink usually reach the family through the   13
women's hands, fear of women frequently translates into suspicion that they are poisoners. Knives, in the traditional view, are "male" weapons. They are wielded aggressively, and they pertain to the masculine realm of fighting, war, and the hunt; they are essential for carving meat. From a symbolic point of view, knives are phallic. We have seen how in medieval Europe, men were supposed to cut for their womenfolk at table. Poison, on the other hand, is a secretive, sneaky way of killing anyone, in addition to which it is often liquid, and administered in food—all of which makes poison a peculiarly "female" weapon, certainly in the folklore and mythology of all races, and possibly in fact as well. Fear of poison can strengthen the pressure upon men not to rove, but stay with their families: they might eat only what is prepared for them by their wives or mothers, or by women otherwise in their control.

Alcoholic drinks, like knives, have always been thought   14
especially dangerous in the hands of women, and men have taken great care to prevent their own partiality for alcohol from infecting "the fair sex." Their solicitude has, until recently, been effective: the percentage of female heavy drinkers has usually been comparatively very low. (It is now rising alarmingly, according to Noel and McCrady for example.) Women must take responsibility for their unborn children, and it is certain that heavy drinking during pregnancy can have ill effects. In any case, what was disgraceful behaviour in a man was always far worse if seen in a woman. During the nineteenth century in Europe, women at table were not to ask for wine; the men were expected to keep them supplied. A man would serve himself and his female partner simultaneously: he would bow, then drink with her. Women were expected not to accept wine every time they were offered it. In France it was correct for a man to offer a woman water at the same time as wine, for a woman, says the Baronne Staffe, never drinks wine neat except at the dessert: she always insists that it be *trempé*, mixed with water.

Women in the Mediterranean countries, from the sixteenth   15
century until recent times, appear to have astonished visitors by their sobriety. In France, in particular, men "cut" their wine with

water, but "honourable" French women, if they touched wine at all, "used it merely to redden their water slightly." Wine, these days, has become an object of awe and reverence; the only people who add water to it are those who can obtain it cheaply and drink it regularly, and who pay comparatively little regard to its quality. Women drink it at table as much as men do—but even the most recent of etiquette manuals cling to the idea that men should really serve women with the dangerous liquid, "regardless of the symbolism," as Miss Manners puts it. If the host (not the hostess) does not get up and refill glasses when necessary, then "each man should pour wine for the woman on his left."

"Young ladies do not eat cheese, nor game, nor savouries," 16 states a late Victorian etiquette book. The reason was almost certainly the same as that occasionally suggested for women not drinking: their breath would cease to be pleasing to men. Women still conform to expectations about eating less than men do, and preferring lighter, paler foods—chicken and lettuce, for example, over beef and potatoes. In Japan, women were actually given smaller rice bowls and shorter, slimmer chopsticks. In the Kagoro tribe of northern Nigeria, men use spoons, but women are not allowed this privilege. Among the Pedi of South Africa, in the 1950s, women and children used the special men's porridge dishes, but only when they were cracked and "no longer sufficiently respectable" for male use. Cooking and serving food to the men as they do, women are accustomed all over the world to eating what is left over from dinner; they are often able, of course, to look out for themselves while preparing the meal. In Assam, where pollution rules mean that lower castes may accept food from higher castes but not the other way round, a woman eats from the same plates as her husband, after the men have finished their meal: nothing could make the pair more intimate, and nothing could more clearly demonstrate that she is lower than he.

In Europe, families have often eaten all together at home, 17 though where several families lived in one dwelling and dinners fed a lot of people, it was probably most common for the men to be fed first, served by the women. It was the nobility who took part in most of the formal banquets, and among them women were sometimes admitted, sometimes allowed on sufferance, and sometimes excluded altogether. During the Middle Ages, women might sit in a gallery or balcony especially provided so that they could watch the men at dinner. But noblemen could at certain places and times sit each with a female partner beside him—

"promiscuous seating," as the Victorians were to call this arrangement. Another possibility was for all the women to sit at one end of the table, apparently as meticulously ranked as were the men at their end. At very big banquets there might be ladies' tables, apart from the men's. We are told that Louis XIV would invite particular women whose company he fancied to join him at high table, or have the noblest and most beautiful women seated at his table for him; his wife the queen, who might be present, or obliged to preside over a separate, all-female dinner elsewhere, did not have the equivalent privilege.

From Elizabethan times women seem to have carved meat 18 at British tables; this is a marked departure from the outlook which insisted that knives were the perquisites of males. In the early eighteenth century the hostess often did all the carving and serving of meat at table. Lady Mary Wortley Montagu as a young girl took carving lessons; on the days when she presided over her widowed father's table, "she ate her own dinner earlier in order to perform without distraction." As the century progressed, men would offer to help their wives or daughters in this task. But by the end of the eighteenth century, servants increasingly carved for the diners; and with the arrival of dinner *à la russe* in the mid-nineteenth century, carving at formal meals was invariably done by servants, away from the dining table itself. At family dinners, the tradition has survived in Britain of the chief male portioning out the roast before the assembled group.

At the end of dinner, wrote Emily Post in 1922, the hostess, 19 having decided that the moment has come, "looks across the table, and catching the eye of one of the ladies, slowly stands up. The one who happens to be observing also stands up, and in a moment everybody is standing." The choreography is strict: the gentlemen give their partners their arms and conduct them out of the dining room into the drawing room. They bow slightly, then follow the host to the smoking room for coffee, cigars, and liqueurs. If there is no smoking room, the women leave the dining room alone. The host sits at his place at the table, and the men all move up towards his end.

Where port is served, the bottle on its coaster stands before the 20 host, the tablecloth having been removed before the ritual begins. He pours for whoever is on his right—to save this person, seated in the honourable place, from having to wait until last to be served. Then the bottle is slid reverently along the polished wooden tabletop (originally so that the dregs might be disturbed as little as possible, though all good ports should be decanted before they are drunk); or it is rolled along in a wheeled silver chariot; or it is handed with special ceremonial gestures from male to male, as drinking cups were handed at ancient Greek symposia. But port is passed clockwise (to the left), not as drinks circulated in ancient Greece, to the right. "Beg your pardon, sir," says Jingle in *The Pickwick Papers*, after the waiter has left the men to themselves, "bottle stands—pass it round—way of the sun—through the button-hole [both these expressions are ways of saying "to the left": men's buttonholes are traditionally placed on the left]—no heeltaps [meaning "leave no wine at the bottom of the glass"]." At the British Factory House dinners in Oporto, the men move into a second dining room in order to enjoy vintage port, for fear of any smell of food interfering with the drink's aroma.

The men discuss politics, and sit with whomever they like; 21 hierarchical seating is often suspended at this time. It is even correct for a man "to talk to any other who happens to be sitting near him, whether he knows him or not," wrote Emily Post in 1922: the men are at last among themselves, and rules can be relaxed. The women, meanwhile, are served coffee, cigarettes, and liqueurs in the library or the drawing room. The hostess sees to it that no one is left out of the conversations which take place. By the 1920s, all of this lasted no longer than fifteen to twenty minutes. The host "takes the opportunity of the first lull in the conversation" to shepherd the men to "join the ladies" in the drawing room. When the men arrive, they must cease talking to each other and find a woman with whom to converse.

This ritual performance was commonly carried out at formal 22 dinner parties in Britain at least into the 1960s; it probably still occurs. Americans were told by Emily Post exactly how it was done into the middle of this century, even though at least one American etiquette book a hundred years earlier had professed disgust for the idea. Several foreign visitors to Britain in the eighteenth century had found the custom exotic and distasteful. On the Continent, the company and conversation of women had become essential to the makings of a good dinner party; there was no question of doing without them at any point in the proceedings. Men of polished manners were not supposed to hanker after the kind of behaviour, associated with male company, which could not stand the scrutiny of women.

For the point of the ceremony of women "leaving the table" 23 and men being left alone until they "joined the ladies" was not only that men wanted to discuss matters which could not be expected to interest their wives or be understood by them. The origin of it lay in the heavy drinking and toasting, the coarse jokes and laughter among men which the presence of women might inhibit. The ladies would leave the men to it, and perhaps eventually have to go home alone, as drinking and roistering continued into the night. In eighteenth-century Scotland, according to Lord Cockburn's *Memorials*, "saving the ladies" meant that the men would take their womenfolk home, then return to the scene of the dinner party to drink competitive healths to them. They paired off to see who could imbibe more in honour of his true love, "each combatant persisting till one of the two fell upon the floor. . . . These drinking competitions were regarded with interest by gentlewomen, who next morning inquired as to the prowess of their champions."

Heavy toasting died out during the nineteenth century, but a   24 new reason for the men staying on alone came in with the advent of smoking, which at first respectable women would not dream of trying. By the time the ceremony of the ladies' withdrawal was described by Emily Post, it had been firmly contained within constricted time limits. There had been significant changes: for example, it had previously been necessary for the women to send a servant in to call the men to them—in Thomas Love Peacock's novel *Headlong Hall* (1816), "the little butler now waddled in with a summons from the ladies to tea and coffee." At a later date, coffee would be sent in to the men to remind them soon to adjourn. Later still, the men were expected to curtail their own gathering and show at least ritual eagerness to rejoin the women. Both men and women, Post is careful to insist in 1922, now smoked; women must be supplied with cigarettes too, and the thought of anyone getting drunk does not even arise.

Another idea behind the ceremony was that when men and   25 women were together, they felt constrained to behave very formally; only when the sexes were segregated could they relax and "be themselves." The dinner party, with its newly necessary "promiscuous" seating (men and women alternating at the table), had been an exhausting performance; it had actually been quite difficult, because of the seating, to speak to people of the same sex as oneself. The after-dinner time among men at the table or women in the drawing room was conceived as a relief from having too strictly to "behave." English nineteenth-century novelists often use the separation of the sexes after dinner as a chance to further the plot by means of free conversation, and a male character's arrival from the dining room, his choice of a female partner for conversation, became dramatic expressions of the women's interest in him, and of his preferences.

All through history, women have been segregated from men 26 and from public power, and "shielded" from the public view; they have been put down, put upon, and put "in their place"—a place defined by males. Yet this is not the whole story; and in the long run it may not be the most important story. For women— and men have very often admitted it, in their behaviour if not always in words or in kindness—have been an enormous civilizing influence in the history of humankind. It is not only that the way women are treated in any specific society is an infallible test of the health of that society. Women have also played the role—and it has been with the connivance of men—of consciousness-raisers in the domain of manners, comfort, and consideration for others. And the more men prized civilized manners, the more they "behaved" in the presence of women. The ideal claimed by Americans in the nineteenth century, when the custom of the ladies leaving the men after dinner was found distasteful, was in fact a sign that grown men were ready to think it normal to behave decently even when there were no women present.

Women certainly felt more immediately the advantages of 27 courtesy—"*la courtoisie généreuse*," the Baronne Staffe called it— and accepted the ceremonial artificiality which saw them as "weaker" than men, but also "finer." Women had to be bowed to, have hats lifted to them, doors opened for them, seats offered to them; they were served first at dinner. Theirs was, ritually speaking, the higher place, in spite of the underlying realities of their social and economic position. Women in "polite society" consequently became sticklers for etiquette—conservative perhaps, but also protective of the gains conquered. The etiquette manuals, many of them written by women in the nineteenth century, are filled with comments about male difficulties with correct behaviour, and bristling with advice about how men might improve themselves. They always assume that women find it far easier to manage all the skills and nuances required.

And in fact it has come to pass that in many important 28 respects women have won. Men who succeed and are admired in our culture must demonstrate that they have opted for finesse, sympathetic awareness, and self-control. "Male" vices which men forbade in women, such as alcohol abuse and smoking, have become disreputable in men also—although many women are now claiming the "right" at last to indulge in them. Fighting, swaggering, overeating have all gone out of style; one result of the technological revolution has been to remove the requirement that "real men" should show themselves to be rough, tough, and overbearing: one does not need to be physically powerful in order to control the instruments of technology. The gap between the sexes has closed not only because women have increasingly entered what has until now been the men's public sphere of operations, but because men have gradually been made to feel that they should attain the level of behaviour which previously they expected only from the opposite sex. In short, they have become more like women.

E. B. White

■ ■ ■

Once More to the Lake

E. B. (Elwyn Brooks) White (1899–1985), journalist, novelist, poet, essay-ist, was born in Mount Vernon, New York, and graduated from Cornell University in 1921. He joined the infant *New Yorker* magazine in 1927, writing sketches, taglines, poems, and articles. Along with editor Harold Ross and literary editor Katharine Angell (who later became his wife), White was instrumental in the magazine's growth, success, and influ-ence. Among his many publications, we may note his books for young people, including *Stuart Little* (1942), *Charlotte's Web* (1952), and *The Trumpet of the Swan* (1970); his collaborations, editing with his wife *A Sub-treasury of American Humor* (1939) and writing with James Thurber the humorous *Is Sex Necessary?* (1929); and his revision in 1959 of William Strunk's clas-sic text on writing, *The Elements of Style*, which is still in print. From 1928 to 1943, White lived on a saltwater farm in Maine, from which location he submitted monthly columns for *Harper's Magazine* under the title "One Man's Meat." These personal essays, focusing on White's life on the farm and his relationship with nature, were collected and published in 1942 as *One Man's Meat* (republished in 1944). In the following essay, White recounts a trip he took with his young son back to Belgrade Lakes, Maine, where he had spent many happy boyhood summers.[1] One of White's best-loved and most reprinted essays, "Once More to the Lake," was first published in *Harper's Magazine* in October, 1941.

■　　　　　　　　　　　　　　　　　　　　　　　　　　　■

One summer, along about 1904, my father rented a camp on a   1
lake in Maine and took us all there for the month of August. We all got ringworm from some kittens and had to rub Pond's Extract on our arms and legs night and morning, and my father rolled over in a canoe with all his clothes on; but outside of that the vacation was a success and from then on none of us ever thought there was any place in the world like that lake in Maine. We re-turned summer after summer—always on August 1st for one month. I have since become a salt-water man, but sometimes in

---

[1] White describes these vacations vividly in his Introduction to his *Letters*, edited by Dorothy Lobrano Guth. In one of these letters, in fact, White describes this particular vacation trip, in July, 1941, with his son.

summer there are days when the restlessness of the tides and the fearful cold of the sea water and the incessant wind which blows across the afternoon and into the evening make me wish for the placidity of a lake in the woods. A few weeks ago this feeling got so strong I bought myself a couple of bass hooks and a spinner and returned to the lake where we used to go, for a week's fishing and to revisit old haunts.

I took along my son, who had never had any fresh water up 2 his nose and who had seen lily pads only from train windows. On the journey over to the lake I began to wonder what it would be like. I wondered how time would have marred this unique, this holy spot—the coves and streams, the hills that the sun set behind, the camps and the paths behind the camps. I was sure the tarred road would have found it out and I wondered in what other ways it would be desolated. It is strange how much you can remember about places like that once you allow your mind to return into the grooves which lead back. You remember one thing, and that suddenly reminds you of another thing. I guess I remembered clearest of all the early mornings, when the lake was cool and motionless, remembered how the bedroom smelled of the lumber it was made of and of the wet woods whose scent entered through the screen. The partitions in the camp were thin and did not extend clear to the top of the rooms, and as I was always the first up I would dress softly so as not to wake the others, and sneak out into the sweet outdoors and start out in the canoe, keeping close along the shore in the long shadows of the pines. I remembered being very careful never to rub my paddle against the gunwale for fear of disturbing the stillness of the cathedral.

The lake had never been what you would call a wild lake. 3 There were cottages sprinkled around the shores, and it was in farming country although the shores of the lake were quite heavily wooded. Some of the cottages were owned by nearby farmers, and you would live at the shore and eat your meals at the farmhouse. That's what our family did. But although it wasn't wild, it was a fairly large and undisturbed lake and there were places in it which, to a child at least, seemed infinitely remote and primeval.

I was right about the tar: it led to within half a mile of the 4 shore. But when I got back there, with my boy, and we settled into a camp near a farmhouse and into the kind of summertime I had known, I could tell that it was going to be pretty much the same as it had been before—I knew it, lying in bed the first morning, smelling the bedroom, and hearing the boy sneak quietly out and go off along the shore in a boat. I began to sustain the illusion that he was I, and therefore, by simple transposition, that I was my father. This sensation persisted, kept cropping up all the time we were there. It was not an entirely new feeling, but in this setting it grew much stronger. I seemed to be living a dual existence. I would be in the middle of some simple act, I would be picking up a bait box or laying down a table fork, or I would be saying something, and suddenly it would be not I but my father who was saying the words or making the gesture. It gave me a creepy sensation.

We went fishing the first morning. I felt the same damp moss 5 covering the worms in the bait can, and saw the dragonfly alight on the tip of my rod as it hovered a few inches from the surface of the water. It was the arrival of this fly that convinced me beyond any doubt that everything was as it always had been, that the years were a mirage and there had been no years. The small waves were the same, chucking the rowboat under the chin as we fished at anchor, and the boat was the same boat, the same color green and the ribs broken in the same places, and under the floor-boards the same fresh-water leavings and débris—the dead helgramite, the wisps of moss, the rusty discarded fishhook, the dried blood from yesterday's catch. We stared silently at the tips of our rods, at the dragonflies that came and went. I lowered the tip of mine into the water, tentatively, pensively dislodging the fly, which darted two feet away, poised, darted two feet back, and came to rest again a little farther up the rod. There had been no years between the ducking of this dragonfly and the other one—the one that was part of memory. I looked at the boy, who was silently watching his fly, and it was my hands that held his rod, my eyes watching. I felt dizzy and didn't know which rod I was at the end of.

We caught two bass, hauling them in briskly as though they 6 were mackerel, pulling them over the side of the boat in a businesslike manner without any landing net, and stunning them with a blow on the back of the head. When we got back for a swim before lunch, the lake was exactly where we had left it, the same number of inches from the dock, and there was only the merest suggestion of a breeze. This seemed an utterly enchanted sea, this lake you could leave to its own devices for a few hours and come back to, and find that it had not stirred, this constant and trustworthy body of water. In the shallows, the dark, water-soaked sticks and twigs, smooth and old, were undulating in clusters on the bottom against the clean ribbed sand, and the track of the mussel was plain. A school of minnows swam by, each minnow with its small individual shadow, doubling the attendance, so clear and sharp in the sunlight. Some of the other campers were in swimming, along the shore, one of them with a cake of soap, and the water felt thin and clear and unsubstantial. Over the years there had been this person with the cake of soap, this cultist, and there he was. There had been no years.

Up to the farmhouse to dinner through the teeming, dusty   7
field, the road under our sneakers was only a two-track road. The middle track was missing, the one with the marks of the hooves and the splotches of dried, flaky manure. There had always been three tracks to choose from in choosing which track to walk in; now the choice was narrowed down to two. For a moment I missed terribly the middle alternative. But the way led past the tennis court and something about the way it lay there in the sun reassured me; the tape had loosened along the backline, the alleys were green with plantains and other weeds, and the net (installed in June and removed in September) sagged in the dry noon, and the whole place steamed with midday heat and hunger and emptiness. There was a choice of pie for dessert, and one was blueberry and one was apple, and the waitresses were the same country girls, there having been no passage of time, only the illusion of it as in a dropped curtain—the waitresses were still fifteen; their hair had been washed, that was the only difference—they had been to the movies and seen the pretty girls with the clean hair.

Summertime, oh summertime, pattern of life indelible, the   8
fadeproof lake, the woods unshatterable, the pasture with the sweetfern and the juniper forever and ever, summer without end; this was the background, and the life along the shore was the design, the cottages with their innocent and tranquil design, their tiny docks with the flagpole and the American flag floating against the white clouds in the blue sky, the little paths over the roots of the trees leading from camp to camp and the paths leading back to the outhouses and the can of lime for sprinkling, and at the souvenir counters at the store the miniature birch-bark canoes and the post cards that showed things looking a little better than they looked. This was the American family at play, escaping the city heat, wondering whether the newcomers in the

camp at the head of the cove were "common" or "nice," wondering whether it was true that the people who drove up for Sunday dinner at the farmhouse were turned away because there wasn't enough chicken.

It seemed to me, as I kept remembering all this, that those 9 times and those summers had been infinitely precious and worth saving. There had been jollity and peace and goodness. The arriving (at the beginning of August) had been so big a business in itself, at the railway station the farm wagon drawn up, the first smell of the pine-laden air, the first glimpse of the smiling farmer, and the great importance of the trunks and your father's enormous authority in such matters, and the feel of the wagon under you for the long ten-mile haul, and at the top of the last long hill catching the first view of the lake after eleven months of not seeing this cherished body of water. The shouts and cries of the other campers when they saw you, and the trunks to be unpacked, to give up their rich burden. (Arriving was less exciting nowadays, when you sneaked up in your car and parked it under a tree near the camp and took out the bags and in five minutes it was all over, no fuss, no loud wonderful fuss about trunks.)

Peace and goodness and jollity. The only thing that was 10 wrong now, really, was the sound of the place, an unfamiliar nervous sound of the outboard motors. This was the note that jarred, the one thing that would sometimes break the illusion and set the years moving. In those other summertimes all motors were inboard; and when they were at a little distance, the noise they made was a sedative, an ingredient of summer sleep. They were one-cylinder and two-cylinder engines, and some were make-and-break and some were jump-spark, but they all made a sleepy sound across the lake. The one-lungers throbbed and fluttered, and the twin-cylinder ones purred and purred, and that was a quiet sound too. But now the campers all had outboards. In the daytime, in the hot mornings, these motors made a petulant, irritable sound; at night, in the still evening when the afterglow lit the water, they whined about one's ears like mosquitoes. My boy loved our rented outboard, and his great desire was to achieve singlehanded mastery over it, and authority, and he soon learned the trick of choking it a little (but not too much), and the adjustment of the needle valve. Watching him I would remember the things you could do with the old one-cylinder engine with the heavy flywheel, how you could have it eating out of your hand if you got really close to it

spiritually. Motor boats in those days didn't have clutches, and
you would make a landing by shutting off the motor at the
proper time and coasting in with a dead rudder. But there was
a way of reversing them, if you learned the trick, by cutting the
switch and putting it on again exactly on the final dying
revolution of the flywheel, so that it would kick back against
compression and begin reversing. Approaching a dock in a
strong following breeze, it was difficult to slow up sufficiently by
the ordinary coasting method, and if a boy felt he had complete
mastery over his motor, he was tempted to keep it running
beyond its time and then reverse it a few feet from the dock. It
took a cool nerve, because if you threw the switch a twentieth of
a second too soon you would catch the flywheel when it still
had speed enough to go up past center, and the boat would leap
ahead, charging bull-fashion at the dock.

We had a good week at the camp. The bass were biting well   11
and the sun shone endlessly, day after day. We would be tired at
night and lie down in the accumulated heat of the little bedrooms
after the long hot day and the breeze would stir almost
imperceptibly outside and the smell of the swamp drift through
the rusty screens. Sleep would come easily and in the morning the
red squirrel would be on the roof, tapping out his gay routine. I
kept remembering everything, lying in bed in the morning—the
small steamboat that had a long rounded stem like the lip of a
Ubangi, and how quietly she ran on the moonlight sails, when
the older boys played their mandolins and the girls sang and we
ate doughnuts dipped in sugar, and how sweet the music was
on the water in the shining night, and what it had felt like to
think about girls then. After breakfast we would go up to the
store and the things were in the same place—the minnows in a
bottle, the plugs and spinners disarranged and pawed over by
the youngsters from the boys' camp, the fig newtons and the
Beeman's gum. Outside, the road was tarred and cars stood in
front of the store. Inside, all was just as it had always been, except
there was more Coca-Cola and not so much Moxie and root beer
and birch beer and sarsaparilla. We would walk out with a bottle
of pop apiece and sometimes the pop would backfire up our
noses and hurt. We explored the streams, quietly, where the
turtles slid off the sunny logs and dug their way into the soft
bottom; and we lay on the town wharf and fed worms to the
tame bass. Everywhere we went I had trouble making out which
was I, the one walking at my side, the one walking in my pants.

One afternoon while we were there at that lake a 12
thunderstorm came up. It was like the revival of an old melodrama
that I had seen long ago with childish awe. The second-act climax
of the drama of the electrical disturbance over a lake in America
had not changed in any important respect. This was the big scene,
still the big scene. The whole thing was so familiar, the first feeling
of oppression and heat and a general air around camp of not
wanting to go very far away. In midafternoon (it was all the same)
a curious darkening of the sky, and a lull in everything that had
made life tick; and then the way the boats suddenly swung the
other way at their moorings with the coming of a breeze out of
the new quarter, and the premonitory rumble. Then the kettle
drum, then the snare, then the bass drum and cymbals, then
crackling light against the dark, and the gods grinning and licking
their chops in the hills. Afterward the calm, the rain steadily
rustling in the calm lake, the return of light and hope and spirits,
and the campers running out in joy and relief to go swimming in
the rain, their bright cries perpetuating the deathless joke about
how they were getting simply drenched, and the children
screaming with delight at the new sensation of bathing in the rain,
and the joke about getting drenched linking the generations in a
strong indestructible chain. And the comedian who waded in
carrying an umbrella.

When the others went swimming my son said he was going 13
in too. He pulled his dripping trunks from the line where they had
hung all through the shower, and wrung them out. Languidly,
and with no thought of going in, I watched him, his hard little
body, skinny and bare, saw him wince slightly as he pulled up
around his vitals the small, soggy, icy garment. As he buckled
the swollen belt suddenly my groin felt the chill of death.

Mary Wollstonecraft

■■■

Introduction to *A Vindication of the Rights of Women*

Mary Wollstonecraft (1759–1797), radical thinker, novelist, and early feminist writer, was born in London, England, and, after a difficult childhood, became a schoolteacher. After writing her first published work, *Thoughts on the Education of Daughters* (1787), she travelled to Paris as a governess; on returning, she worked for the radical bookseller and publisher Joseph Johnson, who published her books *Mary* (1788), *A Vindication of the Rights of Men* (1790) and *A Vindication of the Rights of Women* (1792), her most famous work. Wollstonecraft had two well-publicized love affairs, the first with American businessman Gilbert Imlay, whom she met in Paris in 1792 and with whom she had a daughter, Fanny; and the second with influential social philosopher and religious dissenter William Godwin, whom she married in 1797 and with whom she had another daughter, the future Mary Shelley, who, as the author of *Frankenstein*, would grow up to be as famous as her mother. The following is the introduction to *A Vindication of the Rights of Women*, a vigorous argument against contemporary views of women. In the introduction, Wollstonecraft lays out the plan and argument of this most influential of works.

■　　　　　　　　　　　　　　　　　　　　　　　■

After considering the historic page, and viewing the living world with anxious solicitude, the most melancholy emotions of sorrowful indignation have depressed my spirits, and I have sighed when obliged to confess, that either nature has made a great difference between man and man, or that the civilization which has hitherto taken place in the world has been very partial. I have turned over various books written on the subject of education, and patiently observed the conduct of parents and the management of schools; but what has been the result? —a profound conviction that the neglected education of my fellow-creatures is the grand source of the misery I deplore; and that women, in particular, are rendered weak and wretched by a variety of concurring causes, originating from one hasty conclusion. The conduct and manners of women, in fact, evidently prove that their minds are not in a healthy state; for, like the flowers which are planted in too rich a soil, strength and usefulness are sacri-

1

ficed to beauty; and the flaunting leaves, after having pleased a fastidious eye, fade, disregarded on the stalk, long before the season when they ought to have arrived at maturity.—One cause of this barren blooming I attribute to a false system of education, gathered from the books written on this subject by men who, considering females rather as women than human creatures, have been more anxious to make them alluring mistresses than affectionate wives and rational mothers; and the understanding of the sex has been so bubbled by this specious homage, that the civilized women of the present century, with a few exceptions, are only anxious to inspire love, when they ought to cherish a nobler ambition, and by their abilities and virtues exact respect.

In a treatise, therefore, on female rights and manners, the works which have been particularly written for their improvement must not be overlooked; especially when it is asserted, in direct terms, that the minds of women are enfeebled by false refinement; that the books of instruction, written by men of genius, have had the same tendency as more frivolous productions; and that, in the true style of Mahometanism, they are treated as a kind of subordinate beings, and not as a part of the human species, when improveable reason is allowed to be the dignified distinction which raises men above the brute creation, and puts a natural sceptre in a feeble hand. 2

Yet, because I am a woman, I would not lead my readers to suppose that I mean violently to agitate the contested question respecting the equality or inferiority of the sex; but as the subject lies in my way, and I cannot pass it over without subjecting the main tendency of my reasoning to misconstruction, I shall stop a moment to deliver, in a few words, my opinion.—In the government of the physical world it is observable that the female in point of strength is, in general, inferior to the male. This is the law of nature; and it does not appear to be suspended or abrogated in favour of women. A degree of physical superiority cannot, therefore, be denied—and it is a noble prerogative! But not content with this natural pre-eminence, men endeavour to sink us still lower, merely to render us alluring objects for a moment; and women, intoxicated by the adoration which men, under the influence of their senses, pay them, do not seek to obtain a durable interest in their hearts, or to become the friends of the fellow creatures who find amusement in their society. 3

I am aware of an obvious inference:—from every quarter have I heard exclamations against masculine women; but where are they to be found? If by this appellation men mean to inveigh 4 against their ardour in hunting, shooting, and gaming, I shall most cordially join in the cry; but if it be against the imitation of manly virtues, or, more properly speaking, the attainment of those talents and virtues, the exercise of which ennobles the human character, and which raise females in the scale of animal being, when they are comprehensively termed mankind;—all those who view them with a philosophic eye must, I should think, wish with me, that they may every day grow more and more masculine.

This discussion naturally divides the subject. I shall first 5 consider women in the grand light of human creatures, who, in common with men, are placed on this earth to unfold their faculties; and afterwards I shall more particularly point out their peculiar designation.

I wish also to steer clear of an error which many respectable 6 writers have fallen into; for the instruction which has hitherto been addressed to women, has rather been applicable to *ladies*, if the little indirect advice, that is scattered through Sandford and Merton, be excepted; but, addressing my sex in a firmer tone, I pay particular attention to those in the middle class, because they appear to be in the most natural state. Perhaps the seeds of false-refinement, immorality, and vanity, have ever been shed by the great. Weak, artificial beings, raised above the common wants and affections of their race, in a premature unnatural manner, undermine the very foundation of virtue, and spread corruption through the whole mass of society! As a class of mankind they have the strongest claim to pity; the education of the rich tends to render them vain and helpless, and the unfolding mind is not strengthened by the practice of those duties which dignify the human character.—They only live to amuse themselves, and by the same law which in nature invariably produces certain effects, they soon only afford barren amusement.

But as I purpose taking a separate view of the different ranks 7 of society, and of the moral character of women, in each, this hint is, for the present, sufficient; and I have only alluded to the subject, because it appears to me to be the very essence of an introduction to give a cursory account of the contents of the work it introduces.

My own sex, I hope, will excuse me, if I treat them like rational 8 creatures, instead of flattering their *fascinating* graces, and viewing them as if they were in a state of perpetual childhood, unable to stand alone. I earnestly wish to point out in what true dignity and human happiness consists—I wish to persuade women to endeavour to acquire strength, both of mind and body, and to convince them that the soft phrases, susceptibility of heart, delicacy of sentiment, and refinement of taste, are almost synonymous with epithets of weakness, and that those beings who are only the objects of pity and that kind of love, which has been termed its sister, will soon become objects of contempt.

Dismissing then those pretty feminine phrases, which the 9
men condescendingly use to soften our slavish dependence, and despising that weak elegancy of mind, exquisite sensibility, and sweet docility of manners, supposed to be the sexual characteristics of the weaker vessel, I wish to shew that elegance is inferior to virtue, that the first object of laudable ambition is to obtain a character as a human being, regardless of the distinction of sex; and that secondary views should be brought to this simple touchstone.

This is a rough sketch of my plan; and should I express my 10
conviction with the energetic emotions that I feel whenever I think of the subject, the dictates of experience and reflection will be felt by some of my readers. Animated by this important object, I shall disdain to cull my phrases or polish my style;—I aim at being useful, and sincerity will render me unaffected; for, wishing rather to persuade by the force of my arguments, than dazzle by the elegance of my language, I shall not waste my time in rounding periods, or in fabricating the turgid bombast of artificial feelings, which, coming from the head, never reach the heart.— I shall be employed about things, not words!—and, anxious to render my sex more respectable members of society, I shall try to avoid that flowery diction which has slided from essays into novels, and from novels into familiar letters and conversation.

These pretty superlatives, dropping glibly from the tongue, 11
vitiate the taste, and create a kind of sickly delicacy that turns away from simple unadorned truth; and a deluge of false sentiments and overstretched feelings, stifling the natural emotions of the heart, render the domestic pleasures insipid, that ought to sweeten the exercise of those severe duties, which educate a rational and immortal being for a nobler field of action.

The education of women has, of late, been more attended to 12
than formerly; yet they are still reckoned a frivolous sex, and ridiculed or pitied by the writers who endeavour by satire or instruction to improve them. It is acknowledged that they spend many of the first years of their lives in acquiring a smattering of accomplishments; meanwhile strength of body and mind are sacrificed to libertine notions of beauty, to the desire of establishing themselves,—the only way women can rise in the world,—by marriage. And this desire making mere animals of

them, when they marry they act as such children may be expected
to act:—they dress; they paint, and nickname God's creatures.—
Surely these weak beings are only fit for a seraglio!—Can they
be expected to govern a family with judgment, or take care of
the poor babes whom they bring into the world?

If then it can be fairly deduced from the present conduct of 13
the sex, from the prevalent fondness for pleasure which takes
place of ambition and those nobler passions that open and enlarge
the soul; that the instruction which women have hitherto received
has only tended, with the constitution of civil society, to render
them insignificant objects of desire—mere propagators of fools!—
-if it can be proved that in aiming to accomplish them, without
cultivating their understandings, they are taken out of their sphere
of duties, and made ridiculous and useless when the short-lived
bloom of beauty is over,[1] I presume that *rational* men will excuse
me for endeavouring to persuade them to become more masculine
and respectable.

Indeed the word masculine is only a bugbear: there is little 14
reason to fear that women will acquire too much courage or
fortitude; for their apparent inferiority with respect to bodily
strength, must render them, in some degree, dependent on men
in the various relations of life; but why should it be increased by
prejudices that give a sex to virtue, and confound simple truths
with sensual reveries?

Women are, in fact, so much degraded by mistaken notions 15
of female excellence, that I do not mean to add a paradox when
I assert, that this artificial weakness produces a propensity to
tyrannize, and give birth to cunning, the natural opponent of
strength, which leads them to play off those contemptible
infantine airs that undermine esteem even whilst they excite
desire. Let men become more chaste and modest, and if women
do not grow wiser in the same ratio, it will be clear that they
have weaker understandings. It seems scarcely necessary to say,
that I now speak of the sex in general. Many individuals have
more sense than their male relatives; and, as nothing
preponderates where there is a constant struggle for an
equilibrium, without it has naturally more gravity, some women
govern their husbands without degrading themselves, because
intellect will always govern.

---

[1] [Wollstonecraft's note] A lively writer, I cannot recollect his name, asks what business
women turned of forty have to do in the world?

Virginia Woolf

■ ■ ■

The Death of the Moth

Virginia Woolf (1882–1941), essayist, literary critic, and influential novel-ist, was born in London, England, and, as the daughter of well-known critic and biographer Leslie Stephen, grew up in an atmosphere perme-ated with literature and culture. A central figure in the Bloomsbury Group, Woolf began writing in her twenties and, with her husband Leonard, whom she married in 1912, founded the Hogarth Press in their home in 1917. With a policy of publishing experimental work, it became one of the most important presses in Britain, publishing not only Woolf, but others as well, including Katherine Mansfield, T. S. Eliot, and Chekhov, Tolstoy, and Dostoevsky (in translation). Woolf began experimenting with narra-tive and characterization in *Jacob's Room* (1922), and her innovations in stream-of-consciousness writing in novels like *Mrs. Dalloway* (1925), *To the Lighthouse* (1927), and *The Waves* (1931) established her as one of the most important writers in Britain. In addition to several other novels, in-cluding the unusual *Orlando* (1928), she also published several volumes of essays, among them *The Common Reader* (1925; second series 1932) and the early feminist work *A Room of One's Own* (1928). Plagued with emo-tional trouble for much of her life, Woolf committed suicide in 1941. "The Death of the Moth" first appeared in the eponymously named and posthu-mously published *Death of the Moth and other Essays* (1943), a collection containing some of her best published and unpublished essays.

M oths that fly by day are not properly to be called moths; they   1
do not excite that pleasant sense of dark autumn nights and
ivy-blossom which the commonest yellow-underwing asleep in
the shadow of the curtain never fails to rouse in us. They are hybrid
creatures, neither gay like butterflies nor sombre like their own
species. Nevertheless the present specimen, with his narrow hay-
coloured wings, fringed with a tassel of the same colour, seemed to
be content with life. It was a pleasant morning, mid-September,
mild, benignant, yet with a keener breath than that of the summer
months. The plough was already scoring the field opposite the
window, and where the share had been, the earth was pressed flat
and gleamed with moisture. Such vigour came rolling in from the
fields and the down beyond that it was difficult to keep the eyes
strictly turned upon the book. The rooks too were keeping one of

their annual festivities; soaring round the tree tops until it looked as if a vast net with thousands of black knots in it had been cast up into the air; which, after a few moments sank slowly down upon the trees until every twig seemed to have a knot at the end of it. Then, suddenly, the net would be thrown into the air again in a wider circle this time, with the utmost clamour and vociferation, as though to be thrown into the air and settle slowly down upon the tree tops were a tremendously exciting experience.

The same energy which inspired the rooks, the ploughmen,   2 the horses, and even, it seemed, the lean bare-backed downs, sent the moth fluttering from side to side of his square of the window-pane. One could not help watching him. One was, indeed, conscious of a queer feeling of pity for him. The possibilities of pleasure seemed that morning so enormous and various that to have only a moth's part in life, and a day moth's at that, appeared a hard fate, and his zest in enjoying his meagre opportunities to the full, pathetic. He flew vigorously to one corner of his compartment, and, after waiting there a second, flew across to the other. What remained for him but to fly to a third corner and then to a fourth? That was all he could do, in spite of the size of the downs, the width of the sky, the far-off smoke of houses, and the romantic voice, now and then, of a steamer out at sea. What he could do he did. Watching him, it seemed as if a fibre, very thin but pure, of the enormous energy of the world had been thrust into his frail and diminutive body. As often as he crossed the pane, I could fancy that a thread of vital light became visible. He was little or nothing but life.

Yet, because he was so small, and so simple a form of the energy   3 that was rolling in at the open window and driving its way through so many narrow and intricate corridors in my own brain and in those of other human beings, there was something marvellous as well as pathetic about him. It was as if someone had taken a tiny bead of pure life and decking it as lightly as possible with down and feathers, had set it dancing and zigzagging to show us the true nature of life. Thus displayed one could not get over the strangeness of it. One is apt to forget all about life, seeing it humped and bossed and garnished and cumbered so that it has to move with the greatest circumspection and dignity. Again, the thought of all that life might have been had he been born in any other shape caused one to view his simple activities with a kind of pity.

After a time, tired by his dancing apparently, he settled on the   4 window ledge in the sun, and, the queer spectacle being at an end, I forgot about him. Then, looking up, my eye was caught by him. He was trying to resume his dancing, but seemed either so stiff or so awkward that he could only flutter to the bottom of the window-pane; and when he tried to fly across it he failed. Being intent on other matters I watched these futile attempts for a time without thinking, unconsciously waiting for him to resume his flight, as one waits for a machine, that has stopped momentarily, to start again without considering the reason of its failure. After perhaps a seventh attempt he slipped from the wooden ledge and fell, fluttering his wings, onto his back on the window sill. The helplessness of his attitude roused me. It flashed upon me he was in difficulties; he could no longer raise himself; his legs struggled vainly. But, as I stretched out a pencil, meaning to help him to right himself, it came over me that the failure and awkwardness were the approach of death. I laid the pencil down again.

The legs agitated themselves once more. I looked as if for the 5 enemy against which he struggled. I looked out of doors. What had happened there? Presumably it was midday, and work in the fields had stopped. Stillness and quiet had replaced the previous animation. The birds had taken themselves off to feed in the brooks. The horses stood still. Yet the power was there all the same, massed outside indifferent, impersonal, not attending to anything in particular. Somehow it was opposed to the little hay-coloured moth. It was useless to try to do anything. One could only watch the extraordinary efforts made by those tiny legs against an oncoming doom which could, had it chosen, have submerged an entire city, not merely a city, but masses of human beings; nothing, I knew, had any chance against death. Nevertheless after a pause of exhaustion the legs fluttered again. It was superb this last protest, and so frantic that he succeeded at last in righting himself. One's sympathies, of course, were all on the side of life. Also, when there was nobody to care or to know, this gigantic effort on the part of an insignificant little moth, against a power of such magnitude, to retain what no one else valued or desired to keep, moved one strangely. Again, somehow, one saw life, a pure bead. I lifted the pencil again, useless though I knew it to be. But even as I did so, the unmistakable tokens of death showed themselves. The body relaxed, and instantly grew stiff. The struggle was over. The insignificant little creature now knew death. As I looked at the dead moth, this minute wayside triumph of so great a force over so mean an antagonist filled me with wonder. Just as life had been strange for a few minutes before, so death was now as strange. The moth having righted himself now lay most decently and uncomplainingly composed. O yes, he seemed to say, death is stronger than I am.

William Zinsser

■ ■ ■

Simplicity

William Zinsser (b. 1922), essayist, critic, novelist, and editor, was born in
New York and educated at Princeton, earning a BA in 1944. The author of
many books, including *Seen Any Good Movies Lately?* (1958), *Pop Goes
America* (1966), *Writing with a Word Processor* (1983), *Writing To Learn*
(1989), and *Mitchell and Ruff: An American Profile in Jazz* (2000), and the
editor of several more, Zinsser may be best-known for his books on writing non-fiction. He worked as an editorial writer for the *New York Herald
Tribune* before embarking on a career as a freelance writer in 1959. He
has been a columnist for *Look, Life,* and the *New York Times,* and has published in magazines such as *The Atlantic* and *The New Yorker.* For nine
years, Zinsser was Master of Branford College at Yale University, where
he taught non-fiction writing, a course which formed the basis for his
bestseller, *On Writing Well: An Informal Guide to Writing Nonfiction,* first
published in 1976 and now in its sixth edition. "Simplicity" forms Chapter
Two of *On Writing Well,* an indispensable writing guide which, the *New
York Times* has proclaimed should be "on any shelf of serious reference
works for writers."

1 Clutter is the disease of American writing. We are a society
strangling in unnecessary words, circular constructions,
pompous frills and meaningless jargon.

2 Who can understand the clotted language of everyday
American commerce: the memo, the corporation report, the
business letter, the notice from the bank explaining its latest
"simplified" statement? What member of an insurance or medical
plan can decipher the brochure explaining his costs and benefits?
What father or mother can put together a child's toy from the
instructions on the box? Our national tendency is to inflate and
thereby sound important. The airline pilot who announces that
he is presently anticipating experiencing considerable
precipitation wouldn't think of saying it may rain. The sentence
is too simple—there must be something wrong with it.

3 But the secret of good writing is to strip every sentence to its
cleanest components. Every word that serves no function, every